Thomas Schirrmacher
David Schirrmacher

Corruption

The WEA Global Issues Series

Editors:

Bishop Efraim Tendero, Philippines
Secretary General, World Evangelical Alliance

Thomas Schirrmacher
Director, International Institute for Religious Freedom,
Associate Secretary General for Theological Concerns, World Evangelical Alliance

Volumes:

1. Thomas K. Johnson – Human Rights
2. Christine Schirrmacher – The Islamic View of Major Christian Teachings
3. Thomas Schirrmacher – May a Christian Go to Court?
4. Christine Schirrmacher – Islam and Society
5. Thomas Schirrmacher – The Persecution of Christians Concerns Us All
6. Christine Schirrmacher – Islam – An Introduction
7. Thomas K. Johnson – What Difference does the Trinity Make
8. Thomas Schirrmacher – Racism
9. Christof Sauer (ed.) – Bad Urach Statement
10. Christine Schirrmacher – The Sharia: Law and Order in Islam
11. Ken Gnanakan – Responsible Stewardship of God's Creation
12. Thomas Schirrmacher – Human Trafficking
13. Thomas Schirrmacher – Ethics of Leadership
14. Thomas Schirrmacher – Fundamentalism
15. Thomas Schirrmacher – Human Rights – Promise and Reality
16. Christine Schirrmacher – Political Islam – When Faith Turns Out to Be Politics
17. Thomas Schirrmacher, Thomas K. Johnson – Creation Care and Loving our Neighbors: Studies in Environmental Ethics
18. Thomas K. Johnson (Ed.) – Global Declarations on Freedom of Religion or Belief and Human Rights
19. Thomas Schirrmacher, David Schirrmacher – Corruption

"The WEA Global Issues Series is designed to provide thoughtful, practical, and biblical insights from an Evangelical Christian perspective into some of the greatest challenges we face in the world. I trust you will find this volume enriching and helpful in your life and Kingdom service."

Thomas Schirrmacher
David Schirrmacher

Corruption

When Self-Interest Comes before the Common Good

Translated by Richard McClary

Edited and Revised by Thomas K. Johnson

WIPF & STOCK · Eugene, Oregon

Wipf and Stock Publishers
199 W 8th Ave, Suite 3
Eugene, OR 97401

Corruption
When Self-Interest Comes before the Common Good
By Schirrmacher, Thomas and Schirrmacher, David
Copyright©2019 Verlag für Kultur und Wissenschaft
ISBN 13: 978-1-5326-9200-0
Publication date 9/12/2019
Previously published by Verlag für Kultur und Wissenschaft, 2019

Contents

By way of introduction 7
I. The Antisocial Market Economy 11
   A. Introduction 11
   B. Power, the abuse of power, the separation of powers 15
      Who controls power? 15
      Corruption – examples from Germany, Austria, and Switzerland 16
      Corruption – examples from the English-speaking world 19
   C. Corruption in its historical and cultural context 20
      Corruption throughout history 20
      Is corruption conditioned by culture? 21
   D. What is corruption and who is affected by it? 23
      Definitions 23
      Sub-classifications 26
      Duration 27
      Corruption cartels 28
      Kleptocratic heads of state 31
      Government involvement 33
      The poorest of the poor as victims 35
      Human trafficking 36
   E. Corruption in politics, the economy, and society 37
      Areas prone to corruption 37
      Parties, election campaigns, lawmakers 38
      The upkeep associated with maintaining corrupt officials 40
      The judiciary 41
      Sports 42
      Academics, the media 43
      Churches 44
      The healthcare system 46
      Corruption Perceptions Index (CPI) 47
      The Bribe Payers Index (BPI) 49
      The transparency ranking of multinationals 49
      The Global Corruption Barometer (GCB) 50
      The Eurobarometer 51

- II. **Corruption: Consequences, Legal Situation, Countermeasures** 53
  - A. The consequences of corruption 53
    - Harmful consequences 53
    - Consequences for human rights 58
  - B. The legal foundation 58
    - The legal foundation in Germany 58
    - The legal situation in Austria 62
    - The legal situation in Switzerland 63
  - C. Governance 65
    - Good governance 65
    - Good governance and democracy 66
  - D. Battling corruption 68
    - Possible measures 68
    - Whistleblowers 70
    - Paul van Buitenen 72
    - Systems for providing tips 73
    - A list of demands for combating corruption 73

- III. **Corruption – The Bible's View** 75
  - A. Corruption from the viewpoint of the Bible 75
  - B. A collision of duties in the case of small-scale corruption among predominantly poor people 77

- IV. **Suggestions and Further Literature** 79
  - Suggestions 79
  - Further literature 79
    - Transparency International Reports 79
    - International 80
    - Europe – Reports 81
    - Europe – Books 81
    - Reference books and academic compendia 82
    - History 82
    - The fight against corruption – law, institutional efforts 83
    - Practical Steps for Fighting Corruption 83
    - Good Governance 85
    - Corruption in the church 86
    - Christian efforts 86
    - The Bible and Christian Theology 87
    - Appendix: On German speaking countries (in German) 88
    - Mafia, Human Trafficking 89
    - Law – German-speaking countries 89

Endnotes 91

By way of introduction

By Thomas K. Johnson

Two of my German friends, father and son, have written a book arising from their deep frustrations. They know that Germany and the neighboring German-speaking countries are generally perceived as quite clean in terms of ordinary corruption, getting good grades on the international assessments from Transparency International and other agencies. But father and son Schirrmacher have a different perception: the German-speaking countries are not so clean, and they are angry about it. And they have found enough stories in reputable newspapers and public records to have a basis to say that corruption in German-speaking Europe is not only their perception; it is a reality that has devastating results in the lives of many people and the entire society. In fact, the patterns of corruption seen in the rest of the world, where the truly evil nature of corruption is so widely to be seen, are also to be found in the lands they call home. That, I believe, is why they go back and forth between reports on corruption in the rest of the world and corruption in the Germanic lands. And with consciences shaped by their Christian heritage, instinctively they want to get the truth on the table for all to see, as a kind of confession of sin. This step reminds me of the slow and imprecise but real national repentance seen in Germany in the decades after World War II, a process called "denazification" by the historians.[1] They are not so naïve as to expect a quick "decorruptionification" of Germany or of the world; but again, confession is the first step toward change. Let me add some philosophical color to their account.

Over the last generation, mostly since the 1980s, social scientists, activists, and politicians have begun talking extensively about corruption, and what to do to reduce corruption. Most of this extremely valuable literature is characterized by a type of reasoning I would call "utilitarian calculus." This means that political scientists, sociologists, and economists calculate the negative effects that corruption has upon different groups of people, different sectors of society, and how it contributes to many other problems such as human trafficking, religious persecution, authoritarian governments, drug addiction, illegal sale of weapons, and the failure of humanitarian aid and development programs. This type of analysis is urgently needed, both to alert us to the gravity of the problem and to suggest specific steps to reduce the problem. This type of analysis is made possible by the maturation of the social sciences in recent decades, as well as by the increasing global availability of information. Today one can gather information of amazing sorts from an astonishing array of sources, but this availability is quite new. But this new type of analysis should be supplemented by an older type of moral analysis that was available to people in previous generations. Let me illustrate this in a few paragraphs.

Deep in the human heart there lie close together, almost intertwined like lovers, one of our greatest hopes with one of our deepest dreads. On the one hand, from our teenage, perhaps even from childhood, as soon as we begin to observe the world around us, we see wealth and power being misused together: wealth is used to get power while power is used to get wealth, each empowering the other. Greed and the will to power, or so we fear, are the two powerful war horses driving the chariot of business and the state that tramples over the poor and powerless. We dread seeing this happen to others, while we are aware of our own vulnerability. Corruption is the link between wealth and power; the powerful practice corruption to buy wealth and the wealthy practice corruption to buy power.

But on the other hand, also in the human heart, lies a longing or a hope for something different and far better. In the words of an ancient apostle of hope, "we are looking forward to a new heaven and a new earth, where righteousness dwells." Though greed, corruption, and the will to power seem almost inevitable and everlasting, something deep within longs for a better future. It tells us that this is not the way things always have to be, that things can and should be different and better. This hope for righteousness may prevent us from falling into the cynicism that tries to find our own corrupt little way of merely seeking wealth and/or power, even on a microscale.

This dread and this longing, corruption and the will to power versus the hope of righteousness, each with deep roots in the human psyche, form the backdrop for many of the stories we tell. Think of the great epics of recent popular culture; the examples that come to my mind are the Star Wars movies and J. R. R. Tolkien's Lord of the Rings trilogy. In both we see wide-ranging conflicts between corrupt power and those who represent hope for justice. Such stories command our attention and can be morally refreshing precisely because they find an echo in the human soul. They portray what we have seen and heard with our own eyes and ears; they also describe something deep inside of us that we know, not by observation but by a moment's introspection. We have the capacity to follow the lords of darkness while something else inside of us calls to follow the heroes of light.

This intertwined hope and dread also comes to expression in some of our great literary traditions. As an English speaker, I am thinking of the legend of King Arthur and the Knights of the Round Table, which has had a powerful appeal for some 1,500 years. Regardless of the historicity of Arthur and his knights, one can opine that the moral power of the stories and the symbol of the round table lies in the medieval perception of the internal links among power, wealth, and corruption. If wealth and power were felt to be connected by corruption, who would not long for a hope-giving alternative story of men of means and might being accountable to and equal with each other (through the symbolic round table where all were equal), while bound by a demanding ethical code of chivalry? Though the characters are guilty of the usual sins, the moral code and social structures portrayed a restraint on unlimited corruption fueled by the will to power. The whole legend is a simultaneous call to hope and to moral responsibility.

As the authors mention, our modern word corruption is related to the old Latin term corruptio, which was one of the words used in the Christian tradition to describe original sin, the status of humanity as having fallen from a status and condition of created goodness to a status and condition of falling for all sorts of evil, whether a revolt against God (the story of Adam and Eve) or a man murdering his brother (Cain and Abel). This term placed human corruption within the grand metanarrative of creation, corruption, redemption, and ultimate restoration, so that corruption is contrary to the deepest origins of humanity and also contrary to the final destiny of a renewed humanity. This placed corruption within a narrative which is even larger than the ordinary tragedies of corruption, such as people dying because life-saving humanitarian aid was stolen or selling trafficked children to become sex slaves. An internal echo of this narrative is why, I believe, most normal people have a two-sided reaction to corruption: We may feel a certain attraction in petty corruption (Who would not like some free cash?), while we also sense that corruption is truly evil, contrary to a universal moral law, even contrary to our best nature and destiny.

The spiritual memory which places corruption in conflict with a broader human destiny is not unique to the biblical tradition. Already the Roman poet Ovid, whose works were written before we observe any Christian influence in western literature, wrote movingly regarding the problem of corruption, which some historians see as playing a crucial role in the fall of Rome:[2]

> "The Golden Age was first; when Man, yet new,
> No rule but uncorrupted Reason knew:
> And, with a native bent, did good pursue.
> Unforc'd by punishment, un-aw'd by fear.

> His words were simple, and his soul sincere;
> Needless was written law, where none opprest:
> The law of Man was written in his breast.[3]

Astonishing as these words may be, something of this sort is, I believe, echoing in the hearts and minds of the many people today who are reporting on corruption and seeking to find better ways to reduce its harmful effects. After widely sampling the recent websites, books, and reports responding to corruption, I am convinced that anti-corruption scholars and activists usually stand out as different from many voices in our time. Anti-corruption activists are not completely convinced by the skeptical philosophers who say that there is no difference between right and wrong (nihilism). Anti-corruption activists are not convinced by those writers who claim that distinguishing between right and wrong is entirely dependent on one's culture (pure cultural relativism). Anti-corruption activists are not convinced that the difference between right and wrong is entirely dependent on a situation (situational ethics). And anti-corruption activists are not convinced by those so-called moral philosophers who say that to call something evil is only an expression of my emotions, meaning little more than "I do not like this" (emotivism).

Anti-corruption activists will more likely agree with the Czech moral philosopher, Jan Hábl, when he discusses ethical realism, the claim that moral categories such as good and evil or right and wrong refer to something real, meaning that they are not mere social, psychological, or linguistic constructs or fictions, even though it may be extremely hard to define what these realities are. Anti-corruption activists might even agree with Aleksandr Solzhenitsyn, who wrote somewhere in his great study The Gulag Archipelago 1918-1956, "Gradually it was disclosed to me that the line separating good and evil passes not through states, nor between classes, nor between political parties either -- but right through every human heart -- and through all human hearts."

So listen carefully to my German friends. Listen to your hopes and your dreads. What I have described above as "decorruptionification" should not only be addressed by better laws and law enforcement. It also has to begin at a less formal level of wrestling with the corruption within us and within our local forms of community.

Thomas K. Johnson, Ph.D.; Kt.SMA
Religious Freedom Envoy to the Vatican of the World Evangelical Alliance
Global Scholars Professor
Research Vice President, Martin Bucer Seminary and Research Institutes

I. The Antisocial Market Economy

A. Introduction

In Bavaria one talks about *Amigos*, in Cologne about *Klüngel* (cliques), in Switzerland about *Vetterliwirtschaft* (nepotism). All of this has to do with what in German is called *schmieren* (to grease the palms, i.e., to facilitate the progress of something), *schieben* (push things along), *salben* (to rub with an ointment), *ölen* (to oil), *versorgen* (to look after), or *Gefallen einfordern* (to call in a favor). Alternatively, one speaks of one hand washing the other or of parasitic structures. That might all sound as if it is down playing the practice. However, corruption is not a private problem and is not a trivial offense. Corruption can kill, for instance if inferior replacement parts are installed in planes, if development funds for the hungry are diverted for private use, or if the drinking water supply is overpriced due to corruption and the poor can thus not afford it. Everyone, or at least many people, are affected by corruption, even if they do not notice it or know it directly. Everyone is affected, but on a worldwide scale it is mostly the poorest of the poor who are affected, for instance when crucial funds for drinking water, medical care, and education are lacking.

The World Bank estimates that every year more than one trillion dollars flows into corrupt channels.[4] The elimination of extreme poverty (people who live on less than USD 1.25 per day) would cost an estimated USD 60 billion per year. It is rumored that even within Germany, Austria, and Switzerland 3% of the volume of all contracts is paid in the form of bribes. International managers assume that on average, corruption raises project costs by 10%, but this number could be as high as 25%.

Repeatedly, new sensational articles and processes have unveiled the following: Corruption and corruptibility are also proliferating in the German-speaking countries, across the spectrum from small-time to midrange and to large-scale corruption. Just how far this can go is demonstrated by the example of Rainer Barzel; his expected election as Chancellor of Germany, at the time of a no confidence vote regarding Chancellor Willy Brandt (April, 1972) fell apart in the German Parliament (Bundestag) because two CDU Parliament members had been bought by the communist (East) German Democratic Republic (GDR). It was only the end of communism (1989) and German reunification (1990) which brought this fact to light. "Until the 1980s, corruption was principally considered to be a national problem for less developed countries."⁵ Then the "Flick Affair" shook Germany.

What once appeared to us to be something only known in the Global South or in Italy has increasingly become an everyday phenomenon in Germany, though still on a lower level. The incorruptible bureaucrat, who once used to be a model of Prussian discipline, is a less frequent occurrence and no longer the model for training or for the selection process. Even if the judiciary systems in Germany, Austria, and Switzerland have largely been spared cases of bribery, *schmieren* (to grease the palms, i.e., to facilitate the progress of something) at embassies, in customs and police-related issues, in the affairs of government authorities and in supervisory committees is becoming more pervasive, not even to mention its presence in commerce.

There are certainly also some good signs. According to Eurobarometer statistics, 0% of Germans reported that they have had experience with bribery when it comes to the police (2% in Austria, while no data is collected for Switzerland). The country in the EU with the highest results is Latvia with 8%.⁶ On the other hand, however, there are unfortunately also corruption scandals in Germany involving the highest levels of government.

The Christian Democratic Union Party (CDU) donations scandal in Germany from around the year 1991 was first uncovered in 1999. It finally reached the former Federal Chancellor Helmut Kohl, who resigned in 2000 from his position as the party's honorary chairman. Indeed, he had not personally profited, but he had allowed the CDU to receive slush funds. Up to this day, he has tenaciously refused to reveal the names of the donors. Shortly thereafter, his successor as CDU chairman, Wolfgang Schäuble, stumbled over the same issue when he falsely maintained that he had not known anything about the affair.

In 2005, shortly before Federal Chancellor Gerhard Schröder was voted out of office, he railroaded the Russian Baltic Sea gas pipeline from Russia to Germany through – without revealing to the public a multibillion-euro loan with generous terms which was extended for the construction of a pipeline from Russia to Germany (which, in the final event, was not used). A few weeks after the elections, he received a lucrative seat as the chairman of the shareholders' committee of the North Stream AG pipeline company, a 51% subsidiary of Russian state-owned Gazprom. Besides some sniffing around by the media, very little else came of this. Schröder and Putin became close friends. Angela Merkel's almost triumphant re-election in 2013 can be attributed to the fact that after Kohl and Schröder, she has apparently been able to keep the most powerful office in the country free from personal advantage – even if that personal advantage is only an expensive lifestyle. The events surrounding Christian Wulff and the reaction in Germany demonstrate just how sensitive the German public has become compared to other countries.

Up to the time of the global financial crisis, circumventing laws, rules, and morality for one's own advantage seemed to many German citizens to be clever and understandable. However, through the experience of the global financial crisis, it became apparent that a few people acting immorally could endanger the livelihood of billions of people. One individual perhaps has one yacht more – but mostly not even that – while millions can suddenly no longer pay for food or, in the Western world, no longer pay off their home.

I (Thomas) had two completely different experiences and events which were effectively my personal introduction to the topic of corruption. In 1979, I had a return flight from Jakarta, the capital of Indonesia, which had been properly booked, paid for, and confirmed, as was the flight for the individual with whom I was traveling. When we wanted to check in, we discovered that all the seats were taken. All my protests were of no avail, and we thus spent an unpleasant week of waiting in the middle of the rainy season. Fortunately, friends offered us overnight accommodation. Day after day we experienced the same thing: All seats were taken. My brother-in-law, who was living in the country, enlightened me: When checking in, the counter had two levels. An individual was to place his ticket on the upper part of the counter, while a gift was placed on the counter's lower level. We received our seating assignments in a flash. From the outset, clerks working the counters received a very low salary because it was expected that they would improve it through corruption. It was a guarantee for an almost endless cycle. Was it correct – especially as a "devoted" Christian – to give the expected gift? Or should we have remained indefinitely in Indonesia? Nowadays there are, at least, places in Indonesia where a person can lodge a complaint.

That was 35 years ago, and we are glad to be in "reliable," allegedly corruption-free Germany. Shortly after that, I (Thomas) – then still a student – wrote a newspaper article as an intern about how easy it was to get drugs at certain schools in the area where I lived. In addition to that, everyone knew that drug raids were ineffective because a warning somehow always came beforehand. Shortly thereafter, the department head for drug-related issues summoned me and wanted to force me to reveal my sources. He treated me like a criminal, not like a witness. I had the feeling that he was himself an addict and suspected that he was the leak. In any event, I promptly, and in my naïveté, filed a complaint with the state office of criminal investigation which held a hearing about my interrogation. A few weeks later, the department head for drug-related issues was transferred to a traffic school. I never heard anything after that. In any event, these two different events were my introduction to the topic.

As human rights activists, we chose to address the topic of corruption because of the multi-faceted connections between corruption and human rights abuses. Corruption frequently infringes upon human rights, and conversely human rights are infringed upon in order to conceal corruption. Indeed, a significant part of human rights violations first occur due to corruption or when the prosecution of human rights violations does not function due to a corrupt judicial system.

Philipp Jakob Spener (1635-1705), the father of Pietism, which is the trajectory of belief in which we include ourselves, wrote in 1675 in his major work *Pia Desideria* (*Pious Desires*) about how terrible it is that even Christians gain "an edge" which "make[s] it difficult ... for one's neighbor, indeed oppressing and bleeding him." Old Testament prophets saw in fighting corruption and greed the best manner of protection of the poor and those whose rights are vulnerable. We can only endorse that.

There are still three preliminary remarks to be made:

1. I (David) have studied in Poland, among other locations, and have business connections to China and Korea. I (Thomas) have professorships in Romania and India and know both countries well. These are countries in which corruption is widespread, even if the situation varies from one country to another.

2. More than one-half of the examples come from Germany, Austria, and German-speaking Switzerland, thus the countries of original readers. The rest are examples from around the world. Each of these examples has a small cursive prefix so that they can easily be distinguished from the rest of the text.

3. In the concrete examples we list here, what is generally involved are cases where the results were legal convictions and for that reason were made public. This is also the reason why a number of the cases stem from quite a few years ago.

B. Power, the abuse of power, the separation of powers

Who controls power?

"Power corrupts; absolute power corrupts absolutely." That is a shortened statement by the British historian Lord Acton (1834-1902) from 150 years ago. As a Christian, Acton believed that people are evil and that no one can truly be trusted: ". . . my dogma is . . . the general wickedness of men in authority . . ."[7] This is why power has to be shared, limited by time restrictions, and controlled. Since the 17th century, the teaching of original sin had led increasingly to the political conclusion of installing a separation of powers, which can be traced back to John Calvin (1509-1564). Today it is often forgotten that the separation of powers should materially serve to combat corruption.

Therefore, one does not have to wait until there is a particular case of corruption before something is done to reduce it. Rather, all systems should be set up from the beginning in a way that takes corruption into account and protects against it. Surely there are many people who are not corrupt, but they will not be bothered by such preventative measures, checks, and punishments. Everyone else should know from the start that corruption is expected and, for that reason, resolute steps will be undertaken to control it.

Greed leads to corruption when it is coupled with the power to exploit others and create illegitimate advantages. Greedy and corrupt attitudes lead to corrupt behavior, which in turn makes an individual more corrupt and destroys an individual's entire character. Success screams for a repeat, and inhibitions fall, not only in relation to corruption itself. The necessity of separating power does not only apply to politics. Rather, it applies to all areas of life. Wherever individual companies such as Google become too powerful and no longer have to share their power, the consequences are the abuse of power, manipulation, and corruption on a large scale.

Power plays a central role in all forms of human coexistence. Without power, nothing could be organized, configured, and changed for the good. However, power also means that possible courses of action are always limited for other people. For the sake of people's freedom, this may only happen when it is unavoidable, well-conceived, justified, and for the benefit of everyone. Power must not be used in order to pursue egotistical interests at the cost of others' freedom.

"Whether power operates constructively or destructively depends decidedly upon whether a differentiation can be made between its being used in a manner that is 'subject-related' (*sachbezogen*) or in an 'ego-related' (*ichhaft*) manner, in the form of differentiation made by the individual psychologist Fritz Künkel (1889-1956). When something is 'subject-related,' it reflects the employment of power when the intention is support of the development of community. Thus, it involves building something up, moving developments forward, translating ideas into reality as well as defending something worthwhile. In contrast, something is 'ego-related' when the intention is directed against community – thus, when it is used in order to place oneself above others, used in order to make others small, and to destroy that which is valuable. This is immediately sensed by the environment. The constructive exercise of power is often hardly perceived, or it is sensed to be a 'benevolent ordering hand' and is welcomed. In contrast, the devaluing character of an ego-related exercise of power polarizes endeavors."[8]

Corruption – examples from Germany, Austria, and Switzerland

Here are some examples of small-scale and large-scale corruption from the German-speaking countries.

An example from Berlin/Dresden – official documents: 2,000 people in Berlin had to give their driver's license back recently and re-acquire them since German technical inspection association (Technische Überwachungsverein, or TÜV) employees had for years helped on the oral examination in exchange for cash. And in Dresden, two German foreign ministry employees acquired residence permits for Vietnamese individuals in exchange for cash.

An example from Hamburg – investigation by the Senate: The Hamburg Senate's Bureau of the Interior ordered a comprehensive study in 2009. It was shown that companies had paid €4.47 million in bribes and had thereby received benefits amounting to €35.26 million. If such investigations were conducted everywhere, one could arguably extrapolate that there are similar circumstances all around the Germany.

An example from Munich – Allianz Stadium: Karl-Heinz Wildmoser, Jr., the General Manager of TSV 1860 Munich (a German soccer team), was sentenced to four and one-half years' imprisonment because he and his father, the president of the team's association, received €2.8 million at the time of the building of the Allianz Stadium for providing the Austrian construction company, Alpine-Mayreder Bau Salzburg GmbH, with information necessary in order to receive the construction contract in the amount of €280 million.

I. The Antisocial Market Economy

An example from Bavaria – Formula 1 shares: The Formula 1 chief Bernie Ecclestone was facing charges at the time of the writing of the German version of this book (April 2014) on counts of bribery and breach of trust in a serious case before the District Court (*Landgericht*) in Munich. Ecclestone had arranged for the BayernLB Chairman Gerhard Gribkowsky to receive close to US $44 million in order for the bank to support the sale of a block of shares to the favored Luxemburg financial investor CVC, which in turn paid Ecclestone a USD 41 million commission.

An Example from Germany – VW: In 2005, it became known that the top management of Volkswagen (VW) had for decades bribed members of the workers' council (*Betriebsrat*) with financial benefits, luxury travel, and visits to brothels around the world. There were convictions on both the employer and union sides. The prior board member in charge of personnel, Peter Hartz, was sentenced to a period of probation, the prior chairman of the general works council, Klaus Volkert was sentenced to a prison term of almost three years in 2008/2009. VW had paid hundreds of thousands of euros for Volkert's Brazilian mistress. Investigations against VW began rather randomly: It came to the attention of the State Criminal Police Office (*Landeskriminalamt*) that the individuals observing a brothel did not provide reports for Wednesdays. The reason given was that in each case a member of the VW board brought VW workers' council members and union members to the brothel. The underhanded cooperation between the ruling Social Democratic Party of Germany (*Sozialdemokratische Partei Deutschlands*) and VW began immediately after World War II and was simple because the state was a part owner of VW. It was under the administrations of Gerhard Schröder und Christian Wulff that the travel and brothel affair had its climax, whereby Schröder came away from the affair untainted. This was the case even though Peter Hartz was still one of Schröder's closest advisors after Schröder had already become the German Chancellor.

An example from Germany – Siemens: In 2006, the Munich district attorney's office conducted a large-scale raid at Siemens, Europe's largest technology group. The results of the investigations shook this international group and swept away practically the entire management team. American lawyers also combed through the company. After all, what was at issue were payments of bribes amounting to an estimated €1.3 billion between 2000 and 2006. All of this led to fines of approximately €1 billion in the USA and Germany in 2008. For the first time, it became apparent in the German-speaking realm that the lack of prevention of corruption could endanger the reputation of large companies and their very existence.

An example from Switzerland – the choice of judges: Judges in Switzerland are in each case sponsored by a large party and then placed into office by a group of colluding parties. They pay a set percentage of their salaries as a so-called "mandate tax" (*Mandatsteuer*) to "their" party. If they do not do this, they are threatened with not being nominated for an additional term. That this does not occur voluntarily is demonstrated by the fact that most judges refuse to make the payment if they are already in their final term of office.⁹

> *Well known large-scale incidents of corruption in Germany*
> - **The Lockheed Scandal** (Bribes paid by Lockheed to the ministries of defense in a number of countries in connection with the purchase of the Starfighter F 104 in 1961); investigated by a fact-finding committee of the German Parliament (*Bundestag*) in 1978-1979 and an investigating committee of the US Congress; imprisonment of the Italian Defense Minister in 1979 and the Japanese Prime Minister in 1983; the resignation of Prince Bernhard of the Netherlands from almost all offices in 1976.
> - **The Flick Party Donations Affair** (1975-1981); sentencing in 1987, among others, of the prior Federal Minister for Economic Affairs (*Bundeswirtschaftsminister*) Hans Friderichs und Otto Graf Lambsdorff (both members of the Free Democratic Party [*Freie Demokratische Partei Deutschlands*, or FDP).
> - **The Siemens Scandal** [see above] (2000-2006, uncovered beginning in 2006); a total of US $ 1 billion in fines in the USA and Germany; no individuals sentenced; proceedings against the chairman of the board of Siemens were terminated in 2011.
> - **The VW General Works Council** [see above] (approx. 1990-2005; sentencing of Peter Hartz, Klaus Volkert, and others 2007-2009).
> - **The CDU Contributions Affair** [see chapter entitled "An Introduction to the Topic"] (1991 ff., uncovered beginning in 1999); resignation of Helmut Kohl as the honorary chairman of the Christian Democratic Union Party (*Christlich Demokratische Union*, or CDU) in 2000.
> - **The Cologne Contributions Affair** [see Part II, the chapter entitled "The Consequences of Corruption"] (1994-1999); the Cologne SPD Party received donations from Hellmut Trienekens in order to "promote" the construction of a waste incineration plant; sentencing took place in 2008.

I. The Antisocial Market Economy   19

> *Well known large-scale incidents of corruption in Austria*[10]
> - **The Telekom Affair**: involved illegal contributions to the Freedom Party of Austria (*Freiheitliche Partei Österreichs*, or FPÖ); corrupt awarding of contracts by two Vice Chancellors of Austria (FPÖ) (2000-2006); the resignation of the former Chancellor Wolfgang Schüssel (Austrian People's Party/*Österreichische Volkspartei*, or ÖVP) from his office with the National Council in 2011.
> - **The Tetron Affair** (2003): Money laundering and the payment of kickbacks; occurred in connection with a conversion announced by the Ministry of the Interior to convert to a new digital radio network for authorities and emergency personnel benefitting employees of the Federal Ministry of the Interior; has been under investigation by a parliamentary panel since 2011.
>
> *Well-known large-scale incidents of corruption in Switzerland*
> - **The FIFA-ISL Affair** [see Part II, the chapter entitled "The Consequences of Corruption" – Athletics] (1989-2001): payments of CHF 138 million or more to FIFA officials for broadcasting rights; manager fines, CHF 5.5 million in fines; several FIFA officials were indicted in the US and Switzerland in 2015.
> - **Awarding the 2022 Soccer World Cup** to the small desert kingdom of Qatar (2012): Investigations are ongoing.

Corruption – examples from the English-speaking world

Let us continue with different examples from beyond the German speaking world.

An example from the USA – the sale of visas: In the 1990s, there was a tight network between the visa department at the US Embassy in Prague and Czech human traffickers in the US.[11] An employee of the US Department of State, who earned USD 1.3 million selling visas, was arrested in Guyana in 2000. A visa sales ring in the US embassy in Mexico City, in which dozens of customs and border officials were involved, was discovered in 2005.

An example from Canada – issuing loans: An employee at the Royal Bank of Canada was convicted for enabling a metal goods company to receive a loan of tens of millions of dollars in which papers were falsified. He received approximately $300,000 in return.

An example from Kenya – road construction / development assistance: In 2004, 14% of the roads in Kenya were paved. In 1990, it was 13%. Between those two dates lie hundreds of millions of dollars of support from overseas which flowed into the expansion of the road system in order for the country to develop economically and in order to reduce the accident rate and death toll on Kenyan roads. Furthermore, construction is a continual effort, but quality materials are largely not utilized and millions have been stolen. The ministry for road construction is viewed by those providing aid from overseas to be a black hole.[12]

C. Corruption in its historical and cultural context

Corruption throughout history

There has always been corruption. However, it was always frowned upon and penalized. Some incidental information should demonstrate this. Naturally, we cannot take the necessary time in this work to provide a history of corruption and its punishment.

Corruption was condemned in the penal codes of ancient Egypt, ancient Greece, and pre-Christian India and China. The Twelve Tables, a collection of laws originating in Rome around 450 B.C., which was displayed at the Roman Forum, called for the death penalty for corruptible judges.

As far as the church father St. Augustine (354-430 A.D.) was concerned, the corruption of the political class of the Roman Empire was a reflection of and the cause of the downfall of Rome.

The legislation of the Emperor Theodosius, the so-called *Codex Theodosianus*, dates from the 5th century and contains regulations against bribery and corruptibility as well as against usury and extortion.

In the middle of the 11th century, the common gift to a patron, which arose in the late Roman era, began to change. Political thinkers began to discuss corruption in public office.

In the "Imperial Law Code" of Emperor Charles V (the so-called *Carolina*) in the 16th century, one reads the following: "I swear that I shall and so desire, in affairs which are punishable, to let justice prevail, to judge and to adjudicate, for the poor as for the affluent, and not allow judgment on account of anything else, be it according to the person, suffering, reward, gifts, nor any other thing."

In earlier times, rulers and the powerful practiced kleptocracy much more intensively – one only has to think of the French King Louis XIV and his Palace of Versailles – or it was officially part of the system. In the feudal economy, an office always had revenues, even if one had to grant protection to produce revenues. Power and financial and other advantages were seen as a unit. In the 18th century, corruption was systematically practiced by feudal states, for instance by bribing the ministers of other states.

However, this history changes nothing about the fact that criticism of corruption never fell silent and that for their part, corrupt rulers severely punish corruption among subordinates.

The ideal picture of the state (or church) representative only being committed to serving what is just, and what the provisions of the state are, is rather new and emerged with the rise of enlightened monarchs. Originally, the bureaucrat was essentially an invention against corruption in commerce, the armed forces, and politics.[13]

In return for offering the imperial crown to the Prussian King Wilhelm in 1870, the Bavarian King Ludwig II received 300,000 Goldmarks annually from Bismark's secret "Guelph Fund" from 1871 to 1886, with which King Ludwig financed his famous castles. The fact that this occurred in secret, indeed that the fund from which the money came did not officially exist, shows, however, that one was aware of the immoral nature of this corruption.

From the 14th century onwards, "public interest" and the "common good" can be seen to be increasingly used to describe what the government – initially at the municipal level – should do. The maxim "the common good before one's own good" from the French writer and state theoretician Baron de Montesquieu (1689-1755), in his main work entitled *The Spirit of Laws*, came to be used more and more, not only for dealing with citizens. Rather, it came to also be a standard for rulers. The abuse of the sentence "the common good before one's own good" during the time of the Third Reich changes nothing about the meaning of the actual idea it represents. Montesquieu also formulated a separation of powers to ensure that rulers are controlled and limited and so that the misuse of power is either prevented, discovered more quickly, or limited so that it is not as great as in a situation where all the power rests in one hand.

Is corruption conditioned by culture?

Is corruption something that all of humankind defines in the same way and similarly condemns? Or does the definition of corruption depend so heavily on the respective time and society that international comparisons are not possible to make? Asked another way: Is corruption something like torture, which is wrong always and everywhere, regardless of the culture? Or can something like tax evasion only be defined at a certain time and in a certain country and change according to tax legislation?

Surely there are large cultural differences in the understanding of public office, for instance in dealing with gifts and in dealing with the payment of people working for the state. And naturally, there have been significant differences in which types of corruption have been punished and how this has occurred, even if over the course of recent years there has been a vast harmonization of legislation. Nevertheless, apart from doubtful cases, there are many types of corruption which the majority of all of us mortals consider to be wrong and objectionable, regardless of whether they are directly punishable. However, this is seen at the latest when rulers are considered to be completely corrupt, as happens at almost every revolution; then is a strong desire to place uncorrupt politicians in their stead. This shows that even in a very corrupt society there is a general awareness of what should not be and that corruption damages society. Egypt, for example, is a society ridden with corruption. Despite this, perhaps on account of this, Mohammed Mursi was able to become President of Egypt with the promise to end corruption and to care for the poor. The fact that the public already wanted to get rid of him after a year had to do with the fact that he was shown to be corrupt and was more concerned with looking after his own future than the good of his country.

Without exception, corruption is condemned in all world religions, even by those which emerged 1,500, 2,000, or 2,500 years ago.[14] Our historical overview mentions criminal law against corruption from every era. Even where corruption is a fixed part of the culture, it is nevertheless seen as such and is at least condemned with respect to those who rule.

The argument that combating corruption is cultural imperialism, and that one has to accept that there are cultures in which making gifts to holders of office is simply commonplace, lost its penetrative power in 2003 when far more than three-quarters of all the member states of the UN voluntarily agreed to the UN Convention against Corruption. This occurred despite the fact that the Convention went beyond any standards up to that point as far as anti-corruption agreements in the USA and Europe were concerned. In the meantime, 175 countries have ratified the Convention! Additionally, the Convention was even signed by many social-democratic and socialist governments, meaning that this was clearly not a neo-liberal project or a suspected capitalistic project as many have maintained. At the time of signing, there was hardly any pressure placed upon the states. Pressure placed upon the states is now increasingly the case due to mutual monitoring of the states among themselves, by NGOs, and by the media.

D. What is corruption and who is affected by it?

Definitions

Corruption is designated by its secrecy. For that reason, concealment as well as covering up, deception, lying, cheating, and betrayal of trust are always components of corruption. Corruption always involves more than one person who profits from it. If it involves a poor individual who has to purchase a service to which he is entitled, such as medical treatment, it is certainly the wealthy and more powerful individuals who win. If that is not the case, then both sides have an additional profit at the cost of others, which they would not have had without corruption. This is the case, for instance, when a business person bribes a civil servant who is responsible for awarding a contract. One of the two, or both, is in a position of being more powerful than other members of the society, for where there is no power, it cannot be misused. The higher the position of power, the greater the potential profit.

The UN's Development Programme (UNDP) has extended a formula by Robert Klitgaard which speaks about the monopoly of power.

> Corruption = (Monopolized power plus secrecy) minus (accountability, integrity, transparency)[15]

Three levels of the definition of corruption can be differentiated, whereby in this book we are working with the principle of the second level:

1) Penologists define corruption very strictly according to penal law, whereby the term itself does not appear in German and Austrian law. However, it does appear in Swiss law. Corruption is found juridically in Germany and Austria as corruptibility, bribery, accepting benefits, and granting advantages.
2) Following along from this, political scientists and social scientists define corruption as a matter of the misuse of power entrusted to a person for that person's private advantage, regardless of whether the action calls for punishment or not, and regardless of whether the public or private sector is involved.
3) In addition to that, corruption is often also used in an additional sense by subsuming all bad public behavior under it.[16] What still shines through here is that in Christian theology the Latin term *corruptio* is a technical term for original sin.

Transparency International defines corruption as the *misuse of public power for private benefit*. Similarly, but moving somewhat beyond this, is this definition: *Misuse of entrusted power for private advantage*. Private benefit is not always only for one self. It can also be an issue of benefit for a third party or for an organization, for instance one's own political party.

Bribery can occur through much more than just money and material items. People can be bribed with offices, titles, honors, orders, or promotions, with memberships, insider knowledge, or sex. When, for instance, a boss expects sexual favors for a promotion or receives an offer of sex, and this occurs consensually (otherwise it would be extortion), it is not only sexual abuse; it is also corruption.

Definitions from within political science and sociology are somewhat bulkier and define the typical character of a corrupt "relationship of exchange." For instance, Dorothée de Nève defines corruption as "a (i) secret and (ii) voluntary relationship of exchange involving (iii) at least two individuals ... and which sets out to achieve advantages and is associated with violating existing norms and rules."[17] What is central here is thus secrecy and the voluntary nature of the actions. Without the secretive nature, it could be a matter of publicly effective sponsoring. And the public, in any case, never shuns a true gift. Without the voluntary nature of the exchange being involved, one would probably be dealing with a matter of extortion.

Economics often place another emphasis on the discussion. Here is an example: "Corruption circumvents competition. For whatever reason, the corrupter is an unsound competitor."[18] An "unsound competitor" is someone who can no longer participate effectively in the market on the basis of his natural position. Therefore, he tries to compensate for his weak market position by bribery.

The German Federal Criminal Police Office (*Bundeskriminalamt*, or BKA) defines corruption as follows:

> "Criminological research defines corruption as the 'abuse of a public office, a position in the economic sector or a political mandate in favor of a third party, upon their instigation or one's own initiative to obtain an advantage for oneself or a third party, with the occurrence or in the expectation of the occurrence of damage to or a disadvantage for the general public (in official or political functions) or for an enterprise (if the offender holds a pertinent position in the economic sector).' The guidelines for police information exchange in corruption cases differentiates between 'situational' and 'structural' corruption.
>
> Situational corruption refers to acts of corruption which are based on a spontaneous decision of will, i.e. the actual commission of the deed comes

about as an immediate reaction to an official action and is not subject to any purposeful planning or preparation.

Structural corruption comprises cases in which the corruptive action was consciously planned prior to the commission of the crime on the basis of long-term corruptive relations. Therefore, there are specific or mental preparatory acts which exclude a spontaneous action here."[19]

Corruption is itself a form of economic criminality, but it is, at the same time, a permanent attending ill of all sorts of business crime. Clandestine accounts, cartel agreements, human trafficking, organized illegal work, forced prostitution, and insider trading can hardly be conceived of without some form of "greasing the wheels."

> *"The Sisters of Corruption" (a selection):*
> - Simony (the sale of government posts)
> - Nepotism/ unfair patronage (reaching an office through connections instead of on the basis of ability and performance)
> - Embezzlement
> - Misappropriation
> - Pricing fixing cartels
> - Kleptocracy
> - Organized crime
> - Money laundering
> - Illegal campaign contributions
> - Election fraud

We want to address two additional terms: "sweetening up" and "auto-corruption."

Sweetening up: Sweetening up refers to a situation where someone expects an illegal decision or service for one's own benefit, and in advance already provides the individual with something as an "antiseptic" to make him amenable or in order to pave the way. Sweetening up is not punishable since corruption can only be punished if one can directly associate a form of gift with something in exchange. It is often the case, however, that officials regularly receive gifts and in a later case are seen to divulge secrets. It is possible that the case never arises. To sweeten up also means to expect, if need be, a favor to be done due to indebtedness after an individual has helped finance a certain politician's campaign.

Auto-corruption: A special case is so-called auto-corruption (from the Greek *auto* = *self*), which we will not treat in more detail anywhere else in this book. Auto-corruption is where an office holder enriches himself without the aid of another individual, for instance when an official awards a tender to a company which belongs to that official.

Holders of office can found their own companies and shell companies in order to either receive payments arising out of corruption or in order to land contracts for the companies on the basis of the knowledge they possess. It can be a matter of so-called "kitchen companies" (dummy corporations run out of one's own kitchen, so to speak) but also a matter of large independent corporations. In principle, this is still a matter of auto-corruption but is not counted as part of it because the companies founded mostly have their own legal statues and those involved are mostly a number of insiders or at least straw men and women who are involved.

Sub-classifications

> *One can differentiate among four levels of corruption:*
> 1) Individual cases of corruption, opportunistic cases of corruption, small time corruption
> 2) Established corrupt relationships developed over a long period of time
> 3) Corrupt networks, cartels
> 4) Corruption within the realm of organized crime

The German Federal Criminal Police Office (*Bundeskriminalamt*, or BKA) subdivides recorded cases of corruption in Germany into two groups: "In around 85% of the cases it is a matter of structural corruption with longer-term inherent corruptive relationships. The portion of cases from the area of situational corruption, with a proportion of around 15%, lies slightly above the range of the prior year (between 11% and 14%)."[20]

> "Two types of corruption can be differentiated when one looks at the individual offering the bribe. There is either an individual who bribes out of desperation (Perhaps this person is compelled to pay a bribe.), or someone who greedily anticipates to make a profit by using bribery. The first type of corruption is close to extortion. A position of power is exploited in order to extort a special service from a partner with whom one has some sort of interaction. It is a matter of pressured corruption. It is above all widespread in developing countries ... The second is dominant in developed constitutional states such as Germany. One could look at it as a form of corruption which eases a burden. It is sensed by the direct participants – as in an exchange – to be advantageous. Admittedly, it involves an exchange which

disadvantages a third party. Corruption which eases a burden is always associated with a breach of trust."[21]

Fredrik Galtung refers to "systemic corruption," when corruption is a basic component of a system. This can go so far as to mean that the system is even dependent upon its existence, for instance when salaries in the public sector no longer cover the cost of living. Such systems can hardly be reformed.[22]

Classic cartels with few players are found, for example, in the triad of defense companies, defense ministries, procurement offices, and the responsible parliamentarians and politicians. Price agreements and price cartels presuppose corruption. Indeed, in the broadest sense they belong to corruption, but we have left them out of this book.

Duration

> "What continues to clearly be predominant is structural corruption, by which the crime is actually committed on the basis of corrupt relationships in place over a longer period of time. The act is consciously planned in the run-up to committing the crime, and the process contains concrete preparatory actions which are undertaken. This determination is also reflected in examining the duration of the corrupt relationships between givers and takers, by which relationships with a duration of three to five years or longer predominate."[23]

Frankfurt am Main, Germany – corruption at the German technical inspection association (Technische Überwachungsverein, or TÜV) over a longer period of time: For a period of approximately 30 years, from 1975 onwards, commercial demonstration vehicle services (that is services that bring a car to the inspection required every second year and bring the car back) could receive the required sticker for deficient automobiles in return for payment of an average amount of 50 Deutschemark, and for accelerating the process 10 Deutschemark. After proof of the situation was provided by means of a prepared test vehicle and investigations were instigated, there were thousands of cases and 41 people who were charged. However, for others the cases had long since passed the statute of limitations. Many more involved parties knew about this or had suspected this and looked away. The system even survived the privatization of TÜV in 1992. There have repeatedly been similar cases revolving around TÜV. For example, at the end of 2013 in Hanau, Germany, police, in addition to conducting other activities, retested 40 vehicles in order to substantiate charges against two employees.

All the examples in the following section entitled "Corruption Cartels" are also examples of long-lasting corrupt relationships.

Corruption cartels

The capitals of corruption in Germany, which for decades have stood at the pinnacle of far reaching cases of corruption, are Frankfurt am Main, Cologne, and Wuppertal. Let us take Frankfurt and use it as an example of where there are a large number of involved parties.

The example of Frankfurt am Main - corruption in the building department with a large number of involved parties: Charges were brought against 132 employees in a bribery affair associated with the construction of the Messe Frankfurt (trade fair and exhibition grounds) and arose out of suspicion regarding an employee in 2001 on the basis of intensive investigative work. Charges were brought both against employees of the Frankfurt Trade Fair and employees of other companies. In the case of the next corruption affair, having to do with the Regional Protestant Association (*Evangelischer Regionalverband*), there was breach of trust by a bookkeeper and the matter of a fax that was not accounted for. In the end, there were charges against 240 people and 120 companies as well as –as in the case of a number of collective cases of litigation years ago - the city building construction authorities.

The example of Frankfurt am Main - corruption involving a large number of parties: From 1987 until 2003, the Frankfurt district attorney's office conducted investigations into almost 3,500 people. Included among them were three very large cases of collective litigation which implicated the city government with 280 people accused. In addition to this, there were an additional 21 large cases of collective litigation.

The example of the Hochtaunus near Frankfurt am Main - municipal ring of corruption: It has been demonstrated in the Hochtaunus district, not far from Frankfurt am Main, that one can also make good money in corruption in less known areas. The origin of an enormous investigative effort was the building department of the city of Bad Homburg vor der Höhe. The occasion was the transfer of an unusually conscientious accountant from Frankfurt to Bad Homburg. There he recognized a name from a large-scale suit in Frankfurt. The confession of a convicted building contractor provided access to a completely corrupt network or, to be more precise, a cartel. When, after long preliminary investigations, official vehicles of the state criminal police office and the district attorney's office appeared on a grand scale, one of the most spectacular corruption scandals took its course and resulted in a class action suit with about 170 de-

I. The Antisocial Market Economy 29

fendants, among them 30 office holders and elected officials and 12 mayors. Additionally, there were party officials, town councils, association directors and building contractors in the Hochtaunus rural district and neighboring districts. From 189 million Deutschemarks in building contracts issued in the time period, the 5 companies making payoffs received about 60% of the total contracts, i.e., 113 million Deutschemarks in contracts. The remaining 55 companies had to split the remainder. Although the mayor of Homburg did not pay tax on 114,000 Deutschemarks in kickback income, had his villa renovated for 34,000 Deutschemarks by a real estate investor in return for making sure that the real estate investor received an order, and raked in much more on all sides, the city paid 100,000 Deutschemarks in legal costs for him, even though he was arrested and then convicted!

An example from Switzerland – municipal ring of corruption: "As the mayor of Leukerbad from 1981 to 1999, Otto G. Loretan established a veritable empire. His network of relationships consisted of numerous people he had in part made dependent upon himself. He had installed protégés in the Leukerbad Group, which he built up and which consisted of construction companies and other companies. It was his ambition to turn the sleepy resort into a significant tourist location and thermal bath center. To this end, massive investments were made in transportation infrastructure, municipal buildings, and tourist centers. [...] Thus, a large parking garage was built, and its effective costs amounted to CHF 23 million. By means of sham contracts, falsified invoices, and a lack of controls, Loretan and his general contractor Bumann drove the price up to CHF 35 million. The difference went into their accounts. In 2003 the municipality of Leukerbad collapsed under towering debt of CHF 346 million and had to be placed under receivership by the canton. Loretan was sentenced to ... four and one-half years in prison by the Oberwallis Canton Court for, among others, multiple counts of fraud and forgery. A number of accomplices came off with milder punishments. In contrast, the defendant entered an appeal. The Wallis Canton Court, and finally the Federal Supreme Court, largely confirmed the judgment issued by the court of first instance."[24]

An example from Germany – ring of corruption in the Agency for Privatization: A network of longstanding acquaintances from Baden-Württemberg installed an elaborate system of graft in the Agency fo Privatization (Treuhandanstalt, or THA), which conducted the privatization of state companies in what had been the German Democratic Republic (GDR). Companies which were up for sale were sold at prices below market value to shell companies belonging to those participating and then either sold at a profit or financially gutted and then closed. In part, there were nesting systems for the sale of real estate. Participating businesspeople were sentenced to more than 5 years' imprisonment. However, the primary participant, who was the department head for privatization within the THA and had even the director there since 1992, promptly fled to the USA with 5.7 million Deutschmarks. The THA successfully filed suit for damages in an amount of 11.7 million Deutschmarks, but the money was never able to be collected.

An example from Halle – ring of corruption in the Agency for Privatization: In contrast, the Director of Privatization of the THA office in Halle received a five-year sentence for receiving payoffs of at least 4.7 million Deutschmarks for the illegal sale of businesses. For a long time no one asked what enabled him to simultaneously own a Mercedes-Benz 600 SEL, a Porsche 911 Carrera 4 Coupé, and a BMW 750 (none of which had been paid for by him) and how he was able to finance his showy and conspicuous lifestyle.

In this and additional cases having to do with the THA, the most alarming thing is that the system of graft was planned in advance and that the job applications for positions with the THA largely took place in order to put the system in place. The total amount of the payoffs and the damage caused have never been able to be determined.

An example from Colombia – a ring of corruption in the healthcare system: This example from Colombia shows just how far corruption can go to become a cartel if the judiciary itself is corrupt. Under the Minister of Social Protection Diego Palacio, there were enormous sums of tax money and health insurance premiums that went to fictitious patients or for billing completely overpriced services and medications. For these purposes, a separate complex network of companies was established. In what amounted to theft reaching into the billions, pharmacists, doctors, designated social care workers, lawyers, public servants, politicians as well as investigating officials and control authorities and the judiciary were involved in addition to the Ministry of Social Protection. Everyone can imagine that in the end it was the poorest of the poor who had suffered the most as a consequence.

An example from Iraq – a ring of corruption in the UN: The Oil for Food scandal began with the Iraq Oil-for-Food Programme, begun by the UN Security Council in 1996 and which provided for exceptions to the Iraq embargo. In 2003 the UN General Secretary and, more specifically, the UN Security Council, installed a commission of inquiry which came to the conclusion that corrupt offices had siphoned off billions of US dollars. The head of the UN purchasing office, Alexander Jakowlew, admitted to accepting several hundred thousand dollars of payoffs. The head of the Iraq Programme, the Cypriot Benon Sevan, was also arrested.

Kleptocratic heads of state

"About one-third of the wealth of the richest families in the world, 11 trillion US dollars, and almost four times as much as the gross domestic product" of Germany, is in the vaults of Swiss banks.[25] It is largely the consequence of kleptocracy (i.e., a government where officials are politically corrupt and financially self-interested), in which the most powerful man in a country misuses his office in order to move immense sums of money to the side, for instance, by privatizing state assets. Actually, Arab countries belong in this list where ruling families make no distinction between the state budget and their own private wealth and, for example, retain enormous oil revenues for their personal use.

Kleptocracy is mostly linked with clientelism and patronage (taking care of one's own clan, one's own party, one's own ethnic group, or one's own basis of power).

Kleptocratic heads of state – estimated wealth:[26]
- Mohamed Suharto, Indonesia 1967 – 1998: USD 13 – 35 billion
- Ferdinand Marcos, The Philippines 1972 – 1986: USD 5 – 10 billion
- Mobutu Sese Seko, Zaire 1965 – 1997: USD 5 billion
- Sani Abacha, Nigeria 1993 – 1998: USD 2-5 billion
- Slobodan Milosevic, Serbia 1989 – 2000: USD 1 billion
- Jean-Claude Duvalier, Haiti 1971 – 1986: USD 300 – 800 million
- Alberto Fujimori, Peru 1990 – 2000: USD 600 million
- Pavlo Lazarenko, (Prime Minister) Ukraine, 1996 – 1997: USD 200 million
- Arnoldo Alemán, Nicaragua 1997 – 2002: USD 100 million
- Joseph Estrada, The Philippines 1998 – 2001: USD 80 million

Additional kleptocratic heads of state:
- Adolf Hitler, Germany, 1933-1945: according to present values at least USD 10 billion
- Hosni Mubarak, Egypt 1981 – 2011: USD 10 – 70 billion
- Vladimir Putin, Russia, 2000-2008, since 2012: USD 20 – 40 billion
- Yasser Arafat, Autonomous Palestinian Territories, 1996-2004: USD 1 – 10 billion
- Asif Ali Zardari, Pakistan 2008 – 2013: USD 2 billion
- Nestor Kirchner, Argentina 2003 – 2007: USD 1 billion
- Recep Tayyip Erdogan, Turkey, since 2003: USD 250 million

An example from Indonesia, kleptocracy: Mohamed Suharto, Indonesia's President and autocrat from 1967-1998, amassed between USD 13 billion and USD 35 billion. This occurred through an enormous maze of companies which were substantially controlled by his six children (and in part are controlled by them up to this day). Toll roads were among the activities, as were television stations, hotels, many pieces of real estate, and the airlines controlling Muslims' pilgrimage to Mecca. One son received the first cell phone operating license. All of this was largely financed by foundations, to which all companies and all individuals with an income in excess of USD 40,000 annually had to regularly contribute if they did not wish to fall out of the President's graces. A central role was also played by Golkar, the President's party, which guaranteed his re-election. It was primarily financed by the destructive exploitation of forests and via manipulating the banks. At the end of it all, the Suharto family owned 2.6 million hectares of property and approximately 40% of the annexed island of East Timor. Indeed, after 1998 Suharto's son Tommy was sentenced to four years' imprisonment and a portion of the family's assets were seized. However, the larger part has remained in the possession of the family up to the present day.

An example from Russia - state corruption: The enormous corruption in Russia, above all at the level of the state and state-owned enterprises and large companies is, on the one hand, traceable back to corruption at the time of the Soviet Union. On the other hand, it goes back to the privatization of state-owned enterprises, where President Boris Yeltsin played into the hands of a few who comprised an oligarchy. Their power was indeed trimmed by Putin, but only to pass on the power to just as corrupt and rich heads of agencies and heads of authorities who were loyal to him. It is no wonder that organized crime is flourishing (the Russian Mafia). Transparency International calculated in 2005 that a deputy minister's position in Russia cost USD 8-10 million and that in 2006 a seat in parliament cost USD 2 million. A Russian Attorney General's commission estimates that Russian companies pay out an annual amount of USD 33.5 billion in bribes.

An example from Russia - kleptocracy: Dmitry Anatolyevich Medvedev, the intervening President of Russia (2008-2012) between Putin's administrations, made the battle against corruption into a central task of his administration, and this led to many good laws. The success, however, has been slight since Putin is now holding his hand over this corrupt system. If the laws were to be truly applied, the majority of the lower chamber of the Federal Assembly (*Duma*) representatives and most governors would have to be prosecuted and removed from office. Russian civil society organizations are active for this purpose, which for instance have recently placed internal documents of the state-owned company Transneft on the internet, according to which billions of dollars was drained off while constructing a pipeline to China.

An example from Ukraine and Russia: What makes the situation almost unsolvable is the corrupt legacy of the Soviet Union. On the Russian side, corrupt networks are well sorted out and kept under the control of Putin the "animal tamer." Ukraine, in contrast, is a classical example of a highly corrupt society in which practically all the parties are an extended arm of corrupt networks and politicians but where no one who enriched themselves in the privatization of industry has been able to win the upper hand. Whether or not the cases were artificially constructed which led to the nine-year prison term for the prior Prime Minister Yulia Tymoshenko, it is undisputed that she had enormously enriched herself. Truly non-corrupt, democratic powers do not have a chance at present in Ukraine.

Government involvement

In the case of all the above examples, what is involved is autocratically ruling presidents who either held or hold the power in their hands in their respective countries. That is what is essential to kleptocracy. In the preceding chapter, we have already seen examples from Germany and Austria in which the chancellors and ministers, i.e., members of the government, were participants in corruption, thus state leaders who were not the highest authorities in their countries. Let us at this point continue with Indonesia.

An example from Indonesia – government participation: According to the World Bank, in Indonesia there is still today an estimated USD 5 billion in illegally harvested timber which is sold. That amount is four and a half times the amount of legally harvested timber. And up to the present day, members of government are involved.

An example from Indonesia – impeding investigations: Indonesia's anti-corruption authority (KPK – Komisi Pemberantasan Korupsi, or Corruption Eradication Commission), which was formed in 2001, has become noticeable. For instance, it achieved the conviction of 42 parliamentary members and 8 ministers. However, when the very successful head of the anti-corruption authorities commenced investigations into a massive case of corruption in 2009 against the head of the auditing office, he was relieved of his duties by the friend of the target of the investigation, President Susilo Bambang Yudhoyono. Large demonstrations and 1.5 million critical Facebook comments resulted.

An example from Turkey – impeding investigations: Recep Tayyip Erdogan is currently following the same pattern in Turkey by transferring, dismissing, and even bringing charges against top officials he has appointed. The fact is that Turkey, which is officially laical, unofficially Islamic, and even in part Islamist, there is behind the high national and religious emotionalism on the part of the Prime Minister Erdogan a concealed yet shameless self-enrichment of the political caste as ever. In February 2014, Erdogan transferred or dismissed 166 state prosecutors and judges, among them notable state prosecutors from Istanbul, Ankara, and Izmir. According to a count conducted by the Turkish media, from December 2013, when for the first time charges of corruption were brought against certain Erdogan supporters and Erdogan's son, until the middle of 2014, Erdogan had transferred and dismissed more than 6,000 policemen and hundreds of judges and state prosecutors. One can calculate how gigantic the corruption network must be that investigations can only be prevented by taking such an enormous number of investigating state prosecutors out of circulation and by making it almost impossible or even forbidden for the respective successors to conduct investigations.

An example from Egypt – Islamism: There are many Islamic countries which suffer de facto from corruption, and Islamism has not found an answer for it, even if it draws a lot of support from the verbal battle against corruption when it is not in power. Due to the fact that for decades Islamists campaigned for the poor and fought against corruption, the Egyptian President Mohammed Mursi was elected by, among others, the poorer rural population. Yet Mursi was hardly in office when he began to collect power and income for Islamists, to be as corrupt as his predecessors, and to forget the poor. Furthermore, he became a threat for the corrupt army, which possesses or controls large parts of the Egyptian economy.

An example from Islamism – financing Terrorism: Incidentally, al Qaeda, the Taliban in Afghanistan, Hamas in the Gaza Strip, and other Islamist movements, which make high moral and religious claims, finance themselves not only through the sale of drugs and human trafficking but also through corruption by large-scale bribes and by allowing themselves to be bribed.

An example from India – state corruption: A final example for religious members' participation in large-scale corruption: In 2008, when awarding rights in connection with the 2G standards in India, licenses were not auctioned off as is internationally commonplace. Rather, the licenses were personally awarded by the responsible minister – and as a result the national coffers unceremoniously missed out on an income of billions of US dollars.

The poorest of the poor as victims

Let us turn our attention from kleptocracy by those who are at the top to people who are at the bottom, the poorest of the poor, and how they suffer additionally under corruption.

An example from Kenya – combating AIDS: Corruption in Kenya's AIDS Control Council has kept millions of US dollars away from the poor and the ill. The government was compelled to produce an inspection report in 2003 because foundations and states did not want to provide any additional aid. The report came to the conclusion that employees had granted themselves horrendously high salaries. For example, the head, Margaret Gachara, had granted herself a sevenfold amount beyond what she should have received within the framework of the salary hierarchy for state employees. A remaining amount of USD 48 million from Great Britain could not be cleared up – there was not a single record for the expenditures. Almost all investigated recipient organizations were corrupt, indeed members of the Control Council had founded their own NGOs which had only received the money in order to place it back into the pockets of the "donors." Orphanages financed with millions of US dollars had to be "closed" since they were unable to demonstrate that there had been even a single child who had been looked after. And at those locations where those afflicted with AIDS were being cared for, these people had to bribe the employees in order to be cared for.[27]

An example from India – poverty: Corruption touches those particularly hard who live in India under the poverty line and still, in order to enjoy state services such as medical care or education, have to additionally pay the doctor, the hospital, or the school director. According to 2009 estimates, Indians who lived under the poverty line (at that time USD 1 per day) pay 9 billion Indian Rupees per year in order to enjoy state medical care and education services. That corresponds to about € 100 million! The very poorly paid truck drivers pay on average €1,000 per year out of their own pockets at the borders between the states in order to be allowed through more quickly. In general, traffic and criminal police often improve their income at the cost of the poor.

Are women less corrupt in the same way that they, for instance, are less violent than men?[28] There is much that speaks in favor of this view, even if the few studies conducted are in part contradictory because it is unclear whether this is only a consequence of the fact that generally many more men are in positions of power – and in higher positions of power at that – than women. According to studies, however, it does appear as if women are less corrupt if they hold the same positions of power.

In corrupt societies women are, however, much more frequently the victims of corruption. This applies all the more in the case of poverty. If on average on a global scale women are more affected by poverty, the consequences for poor people are greater, and the poor have to pay bribes more often, for instance for education and medical care.[29]

Human trafficking

Corruption within the police and the authorities is a part of human trafficking. One would have to go into detail to demonstrate that in many countries of the Global South the human trafficking network is able to resort to widespread corruption. It is also known in Eastern Europe that the police are in part so corrupt and sometimes they are so directly entangled in human trafficking that victims are in principle not prepared to speak with the police. In India it is rather simple to procure counterfeit passports and visas for other countries for the victims of human trafficking and to have these people travel around the world.

The embassies of Germany, Austria, and Switzerland are reportedly cited as examples. One can imagine for himself how this must look in countries without a functioning constitutional state system or with underpaid civil servants, police, and judges.

An example from Germany – the sale of visas: An investigating committee installed at the end of 2004 by the German Parliament (*Bundestag*) was supposed to clear up tens of thousands of fraudulent visas from the period between 1999 and 2002 in Eastern Europe. The primary catalyst was that the District Court of Cologne sentenced a defendant to five years of imprisonment for gang-like people smuggling and at the same time judged that the German Foreign Ministry had "abetted serious wrongdoing" with respect to the offenses. Criminal networks used loose visa issuance procedures and the corruptibility of the employees, above all in Kiev (Ukraine) and Pristina (Kosovo). Within the embassy, for instance, there were corrupt forces which outsmarted the computers tied to the Foreign Ministry's visa services: Even if someone was on the warning list, that individual still received a visa issued in Pristina. The affair was never completely cleared up because it was primarily a matter of party politics and the responsible individuals in Berlin, not the necessary uncovering of human trafficking networks.[30] According to investigations by *Spiegel* (a weekly German news magazine), visas were systematically issued in German embassies in Africa, South America, and Eastern Europe in return for bribes.[31] According to the report, so-called local staff had been incriminated, i.e., employees from the respective countries in the consular sections were implicated with having systematically issued visas for entry into Germany based on patently false information.

An example from Austria – the sale of visas: In 2008 Austria experienced its own large-scale case against embassy employees, including a consul general who had sold visas to human traffickers in Belgrade and Budapest. The employees who had reported this in 2001 and 2002 were first reassured ("the Minister personally assured himself on site that everything was in order") and then these same employees became the target of investigations. The successor Consul General who wanted to uncover everything was unceremoniously transferred to Poland. The criminal Consul continued undisturbed at the next embassy. That was in Belgrade, where 8,000 visas were issued per year, ten times more than otherwise. In fact, more than 7,000 were issued to criminal networks. When years later it was brought to court, the Consul had already died, and only his deputy was sentenced to three and one-half years of imprisonment. However, the judge ruled that the Foreign Ministry was primarily guilty, which despite obvious indications did not intervene. In 2006 the Austrian Consul in Nigeria was sentenced to two years of imprisonment for the issuance of 700 irregular visas.

An example from Switzerland – the sale of visas: In 2006 Switzerland exposed a three-sided operation between its embassy in Pakistan, travel agencies, and a human trafficking ring.

E. Corruption in politics, the economy, and society

Areas prone to corruption

In which areas of society and the economy is corruption primarily found? According to its report, the Federal Criminal Police (*Bundeskriminalamt*, or BKA) stated the recorded cases of corruption as follows: 48% within public administration, 46% in the private sector, 5% within criminal prosecution and justice prosecution authorities, and 1% within politics. With that said, it is only the number of cases which is taken as a basis, not how comprehensive the corruption was. Thus, in a certain statistical sense, the bribery of a traffic police officer counts as much as an international corruption scandal.

Areas of society with corruption:
- Law (investigators, district attorneys, judges)
- Public administration
- Politics
- Customs duty services, taxes, fees
- Police
- Military
- Prisons
- International organizations
- Multinational corporations
- Commerce

Areas of the economy in Germany, Austria, and Switzerland with higher levels of corruption:
- Construction
- Building administration
- Trucking companies
- Pharmaceutical industry, medical devices
- Arms industry
- Waste management industry
- Real estate
- Advertising
- Guard and protection sector

Parties, election campaigns, lawmakers

As Laurence Cockcroft[32] sees it, the main drivers of global corruption are: 1. financing political parties and elections, 2. low salaries for government officials, 3. organized crime, and 4. multinational companies on "buying sprees" in countries with high levels of corruption. Most researchers fill position 1. similarly: If party financing and election campaign financing are not strictly controlled, then corruption is practically anchored in the political system.

In the USA, the financing of election campaigns for president, governors, representative of all types, judges, district attorneys, and police chiefs are an endless source of problems with corruption.[33] Even if over the course of decades there have been increasingly sharper guidelines, the exploding costs of elections have nullified most of the progress. If the elected individ-

I. The Antisocial Market Economy

uals come into office with conflicts of interest or loyalty, then they are already a lost cause as far as conducting a rigorous battle against corruption.

Germany has in part ridden itself of the problem by what is a globally unique, high level of partial state financing of the political parties. It used to be called election cost reimbursement. Even if the parties in a certain sense decide themselves how much they receive, when voting in parliament on it, this has strongly reduced the dependency on large donors. Additionally, there is a strong tool against illegal party donors available in the fact that a multiple of the illegal sum can be withheld or claimed back without further ado. Indeed, this can also be done when there is illegal activity at the local or regional party level. This should not be taken to say there is not a big backlog. This is due to the fact that the German Parliament is very hesitant to increase the disclosure requirement for its members and for other related areas.

Austria is pursuing a similar path to Germany by guaranteeing election cost reimbursement. The sums, however, are nowhere nearly as high as in Germany, and corruption among parties, parliament members, and members of the government is more widespread.

Switzerland, otherwise often viewed as a model child when it comes to corruption, has gone in what is the completely opposite direction. There are practically no transparency requirements with respect to party finances, and actions taken are not punishable. There is as little a limit set on the influence of large banks on parties at the federal level as there is on nepotism at the local level. Additionally, the federal parties do not have to stand legally accountable for the offenses committed by lower level party organizations as is the case in Germany and Austria. This is due to the fact that grassroots democracy in Switzerland allows party organizations to largely act independently.

At the beginning of 2014, after years of inactivity, the German Parliament passed legislation exacerbating the laws relating to the bribery of Parliament and state parliament members. According to these laws, the corrupted and the corruptor, can be punished with up to five years of imprisonment. It is simply a problem when members of parliament and parties exclusively decide themselves about their special privileges.

Federal, state, and municipal politicians are taken care of by receiving top positions in state-owned firms, such as state-owned enterprises, the lottery, municipal enterprises – and all of this is completely legal. In most municipalities, in addition to qualified and experienced specialists within their own sectors, there are those who are from outside of the field and were top party leaders, who at the end of their careers are rewarded ("taken care of") with lucrative appointments for which they are not qualified.

> *Principle demands for better action against corruption in government and parliament:*
> - Strict regulation of party financing, obligation of transparency, legal accountability
> - Required registration of lobbyists
> - Strict regulation against bribing members of parliament
> - Protection for whistleblowers (informants) – also in politics

Transparency International has presented its own investigation of the situation surrounding the bribery of parties, members of parliament, and politicians.[34] According to that report, there is a great degree of variation in Europe. However, not a single country has successfully regulated and implemented all aspects simultaneously. Greece, Italy, and Portugal have great deficiencies in their reporting and have a high level of corruption in the political arena. In a number of countries, such as the Czech Republic, Hungary, and Slovakia (less due to a lack of laws than on account of a failure of implementation), Bulgaria, and Rumania (at the legislative level and at the level of implementation), the trend has gone in a negative direction.

The upkeep associated with maintaining corrupt officials

Corrupt relationships are very often unstable, above all if civil servants want more and more. For that reason, as a general rule, such bribed individuals have to be well taken care of. In addition to large gifts, they also mostly need to be shown many small indications of attention or want to be introduced "to the big wide world."

Corrupt officials, both male and female, often do not receive recognition, especially since corruption has to be kept secret. A sense of "considering oneself to be important" is promoted through participation in networks and events with important people. For that reason, they are often bribed through vacations, holidays, sporting events, and meetings with "important" people.

It is no doubt primarily civil servants and politicians, both male and female, who have no further career before them and for whom power, influence, and reputation are no longer currencies who attempt to then instead get something in the form of cash or material assets. There can also be a completely different cause. The catalyst for Christian Wulff's rather loose handling of gifts from friends from the world of business might have had something to do with the expectations on the part of his lover and then second wife.

The judiciary

Corruption in the judicial system is especially disastrous, since this in turn makes fighting and prosecuting corruption practically impossible. In the Old and the New Testaments, the bribery of judges is paradigmatic for corruption itself. If judges are corrupt, other corruption is difficult to resist (see part III, the chapter entitled "Corruption – The Bible's View").

> *Corruption in the judicial system:*
> - Naming judges and state prosecutors
> - Influencing legislation
> - Assigning judges and state prosecutors to particular cases
> - Bribery of judges, state prosecutors, employees, assessors, witnesses
> - Bribery of all sorts in correctional facilities
>
> *How can corruption be combated in the judicial system?*[35]
> - Good legal education
> - Independent selection of judges and independent committees for appointing judges
> - Independent and strong professional associations with rules of ethics
> - Promotion according to education, ability competence, and performance, not according to connections
> - Good salaries and retirement plans
> - Objective rules for allotting cases to judges
> - Mutual control of judges and the possibility of removing corrupt judges
> - Also, however, independence and protection against harassment
> - Judicial decision transparency
> - Protection of whistleblowers

Political corruption in particular can only be curtailed if the judicial system is not a part of corrupt networks but is rather in the position, and has the will, to decide independently.

In the USA, the election of judges and district attorneys by the citizens and the related expensive campaigns lead to a situation where lobbying groups, along with their high donations, have elected candidates somewhat in their debt. In Germany, the primary danger for the high offices of judge and state prosecutor is that in the final event the parties arrange among themselves who gets elected – even if this is restrained by necessary academic and professional prerequisites.

Thanks to payoffs, prison guards can overlook deliveries of smuggled goods. It seems that everything can be acquired in prisons, whether allowed or not: cell phones, pornography, alcohol, drugs, and even weapons. And there is much of what leaves prison which should never leave, all the way to orders to carry out a murder. Even if it is on occasion the case that lawyers, relatives, and visitors have a hand in things, it is generally a matter of knowing, tolerating, and even participating in these actions on the part of office holders surrounding the penal institutions, from guards to resident physicians all the way to prison chaplains.

Sports

There are ideal areas within society, such as sports, cultural creation, religion (especially churches), and the sciences where corruption is very difficult to imagine on account of the noble goals (science: "objective truth," art: "finding joy in beauty"). However, at those points where there is an interface to profit, the economy, politics, and the media, corruption indeed flourishes, and "corruption [is to be viewed as] a component of professional sports as well as of the entertainment and cultural realms."[36] We want to single out the area of sports as representative.[37]

An example from the world of sports – major events: The venues for the Olympics, the World Cup, and Formula 1 racing are almost always, to a greater or lesser extent, hustled, and IOC officials seem to become rich in a miraculous way even if they do not receive a salary.

An example from the world of sports – referees: Referees of competitive events in Germany are often invited to visit brothels. Between 2008 and 2011, 30 referees in the Czech Republic allowed themselves to be bribed for €1,000 – €6,000 by premier league teams in order to influence the league positions and to maximize betting.

An example from Switzerland – soccer: "In February 2013 attention was drawn all around Europe to the manipulation of over 380 matches between 2008 and 2011 – among them Champions League matches, World Cup and European Cup qualifying matches as well as a total of 41 matches in Switzerland. Investigations in Switzerland led to player suspensions against nine players. However, the Federal Criminal Court surprisingly acquitted the defendants of allegations of fraud in November 2012."[38]

An example from Asia / Brazil – the world of sports: USD 40,000 was paid in order to ensure the victory of a Thai boxer at the 2004 Athens Olympics.

I. The Antisocial Market Economy 43

The Chinese FIFA referee J. Gong was sentenced to ten years of imprisonment because he received €50,000 from bookmakers. During the investigations, charges were loudly voiced that games that are not manipulated are practically unknown in China. A number of FIFA referees from Brazil have been barred for life for manipulating games for amounts of €3,700 to €5,550 per game.

An example from Germany - sports marketing: Between 1997 and 2005, the company Techem paid over €100,000 to a media consultant, who was simultaneously the Central German Broadcasting (*Mitteldeutscher Rundfunk*, or MDR) sports head, so that Techem's unknown indoor soccer championship, the Techem Indoor Soccer Championship (*Techem-Hallenfußballcup*), would be broadcast on the MDR (*Mitteldeutscher Rundfunk*) channel. From 2003 to 2005, the head of the German Sport Sponsorship Foundation (*Stiftung Deutsche Sporthilfe*), who had been the chairman of the board of Techem, hired the MDR sports head for €45,000 per year as a "media ambassador."

An example from Germany - sports marketing: Up to 2004, the sports head of Hessian Broadcasting (*Hessischer Rundfunk*) required that €20,000 to €30,000 be paid by organizations having their sporting events broadcast to his wife's marketing firm or, more specifically, a company in which she held a stake.

An example from Switzerland - sports marketing: "The ISL scandal took on truly huge proportions. In 1982, ISL (International Sport and Leisure) was founded by the then German Adidas owner Horst Dassler as a sports rights marketing firm in Switzerland which went bankrupt in 2001. It has been proven that from 1989 to 2001, CHF 138 million was paid to high-ranking sport functionaries in order to receive broadcasting rights to major events such as World Cups and the Olympics. Three ISL managers were convicted and fined. High FIFA functionaries were reportedly bribed by the ISL. A court in Zug, Switzerland, the prior headquarters of ISL, decided that the matter could be brought to a close by a CHF 5.5 million compensation payment by FIFA. The names of the involved functionaries were kept secret. In 2011 the FIFA paid a total of USD 29.5 million in 'bonus payments' to its 35 top functionaries, and in the same year it paid CHF 4.8 million in taxes."[39]

Academics, the media

At this point one could follow with examples from the academic realm. Academics, ranging across all areas of specialization, allow themselves to be bought. This is in order to provide apparently neutral underpinnings in a scholarly form for the respective desired results sought by politicians, parties, companies, NGOs, the media, and lobbying groups. Media companies producing pornography have for decades commissioned studies which, peculiarly, always document the harmlessness of pornography while independent investigations arrive at much more highly differentiated assessments. Unions like to have economic institutes determine that their demands benefit everyone, and money is no object for their counterparts. Large foundations, such as the Bertelsmann Foundation, are known for the fact that their studies practically always are in harmony with their political demands.

An example from the world of journalism – automobile manufacturers: Almost all automobile producers give journalists special rebates and have large budgets for trips for journalists. For example, VW is reported to have regularly paid over 150 journalists without having reported this, and Mazda in Europe is reported to have apparently had an annual budget of €10-16 million so that journalists could take trips to Vienna for relaxation and enjoyment.

An example from the world of journalism – ThyssenKrupp: A well-researched case stems from 2011 when the steel company ThyssenKrupp came under pressure as a result of numerous negative reports in the media saying that ThyssenKrupp had flown a large number of journalists from large German newspapers via first class to South Africa and financed a luxury stay including helicopter flights and safaris. What was actually a senseless trip as far as reporting was concerned was well worth it. Four journalists wrote long, positive reports which changed the direction of the wind in the media. All four were silent about how the German Press Council (*Deutscher Presserat*) codex prescribes that it should have been mentioned that ThyssenKrupp had paid for their trips.

In the 2013 Global Corruption Barometer (see Part II, the Chapter entitled "The Global Corruption Barometer [GCB]"), it was the first time that those asked in Germany perceived the media to be more corrupt than public administration or Parliament.[40]

Churches

There is no reason to assume that churches would in any way be automatically immune to corruption or, that on account of the moral claims found there, that it would be rarer. Religious power is as tempting as political or economic power. Wherever large sums of money are moved and controlled, there is the temptation for corruption to occur. This is the case whether the church, or more specifically God, is stamped upon the activity or not. Churches and their employees can bribe, can be bribed, and can misappropriate funds for private benefit. In Germany and Austria, churches belong to the group of largest employers and largest landowners, and thanks to church taxes they move billions. How can corruption be a foreign word there if it is not intensively contended with and protected against?

When Paul collected donations for the suffering church in Jerusalem, he never traveled alone with the money. There were always representatives of the church with him. Paul did not complain that one wanted to insinuate that he, as an Apostle, had dishonest intentions. Rather, he himself organized the control. Few know that this is one of the reasons why collections of cash are counted by at least pairs of individuals. The rule on this reads as follows: Nip things in the bud and always reckon with misappropriation, even on the part of oneself. Make provisions. Indeed, protect yourself against yourself.

An example from India – churches: In India there are increasing numbers of bishops who are stepping down because they have bought members of election committees. A famous case is that of the Bishop and Moderator of the Church of South India, S. Vasanthakumar. He had been elected in 2010 but stepped down after it came out that he had bribed nine bishops prior to the election and had misappropriated large sums of money from church coffers.

An example from Kenya/Korea – churches: The prosperity gospel, which is widespread and primarily found in the Evangelical and Pentecostal spheres, often means in the Global South that bitterly poor people support incredibly rich pastors. An example is that in certain churches in Kenya shaking hands with the pastor costs USD 70. It is often preached that being a Christian makes one rich, but it is mostly the preachers who become rich. There is a list of such preachers around the world who have been convicted by state courts of corruption and misappropriation of funds. Just recently, the pastor of the largest church in the world, Paul Yonggi Cho from Seoul, received a suspended sentence for corruption and misappropriation of funds. His son was given a sentence of three years imprisonment.

On the other hand, it is gratifying that churches and Christians worldwide have not only adopted anti-corruption measures for themselves. Rather, they have also become active in the worldwide battle against corruption, above all where the poorest of the poor suffer under it.

> *The Micah Initiative (Micha Initiative, Germany) / StopPoverty2015 (StopArmut2015, Switzerland) – Examples of Christian initiatives against corruption:*
>
> "The Micah Initiative in Germany participates in the global campaign called 'Exposed – Bringing Corruption to Light.' Together with Christians from over 100 countries, the effort advocates battling corruption and tax evasion by increasing transparency. Every year there is an estimated USD 1 trillion – USD 1,000,000,000,000 – which is lost every year through corruption. The sustained battle against poverty – and in the medium term the implementation of UN millennial goals – is hampered by this to a great degree. However, tax evasion is a major obstacle in the fight against poverty. Due to lower tax revenues, it is precisely developing countries which have difficulties establishing functioning educational, health, and social services systems."[41]

The healthcare system

In addition to sports, corruption in the healthcare system needs to be mentioned. However, this will not be done by means of examples but rather by means of a short overview. For instance, corruption in this area leads to inflated prices, and in the Global South it often leads to medications being unattainable, as corruption in healthcare systems on a global scale affects the poorest of the poor. Forms of therapy and medications are established which do not promise improvement but rather better profits and can result in increasing the cost of aid to the Global South. Corruption easily promotes a dual-class form of medical care by being the way one can receive an appointment or an organ for a transplant operation more quickly.

The lowest estimates assume that every year in Europe there are at least €30 billion, i.e., 3% of all expenditures for healthcare, which get lost due to fraud and corruption. A study of the European Healthcare Fraud and Corruption Network (EHFCN) came up with a number of around €56 billion lost every year due to fraud and corruption. This amounts to 6% of all healthcare expenditures.

In recent decades there has been enormous growth in the pharmaceutical industry worldwide. However, in the 1960s and 1970s there was also an exchange which took place. Scientists as CEOs were replaced by business people and individuals coming from marketing. This had consequences as far as competence in innovation is concerned. Nowadays, research accounts for 10% of the costs and marketing 40%, with the result

I. The Antisocial Market Economy   47

that things are less and less a matter of offering medications which are better or for which there is no alternative. Instead, it has more to do with giving the *impression* that one is precisely doing that while not doing it. This situation fosters corrupt methods in marketing and promotion.

> *Selected types of corruption in healthcare:*
> - Manipulation of clinical studies
> - Disinformation by paid scientists through expert opinions and lectures (technical jargon: "horses for hire")
> - Winning journalists over to produce favorable reporting about products
> - Financially favoring doctors if they prescribe certain products (e.g., by paying for their participation in pseudo-studies)

Corruption Perceptions Index (CPI)

Before we concern ourselves with the available rankings on corruption, it has to be clarified that corruption itself cannot be measured. If one only follows the findings of the police and investigating authorities, everything hangs on the question of how good the investigations and assessments are and how big the dark field of corruption is. Since, by definition, corruption is kept secret and is a pronounced control-related offense that only attracts attention when there are strict controls, an estimation of its frequency and comprehensiveness is practically impossible. For that reason, one needs to approach the topic from various perspectives.

The Corruption Perceptions Index, or CPI, has been around since 1995 and is the oldest and best-known ranking of corruption put out by Transparency International. It can be traced back to the German Economics Professor Johann Graf Lambsdorff. For a long time, this was the sole global index and was criticized because it only reflects the *estimation* of a few important people.[42] In the meantime, Transparency International has extended the CPI by three additional and completely differently structured indices which we will discuss below. 0 points indicate complete corruption. 100 points indicate the complete absence of corruption. Data relating to 177 countries was gathered in 2013, and only a few countries are at the top of the list. Two-thirds of the countries have fewer than 50 points. For a long time, Germany has found itself between the 12th and 15th position. Between the years 2008 and 2013, the top three spots were almost always taken by Denmark, New Zealand, and Finland, followed by Singapore and Sweden, which prior to that had at times held the first two positions. Since 2008, the last positions have almost always been taken by Somalia, North Korea, and Afghanistan.

Transparency International Germany has written the following about this on their website: "The Index consists of various expert surveys and measures the corruption perceived by politicians and civil servants." "It is a compiled index which rests upon various surveys and investigations which have been conducted by nine independent organizations. Business people as well as country analysts were asked and surveys with citizens domestically and internationally were included." "On a scale from 0 (a high degree of perceived corruption) to 100 (no perceived corruption), Germany received 78 points. With that said, the Federal Republic of Germany ranked 12. Among European countries, Denmark (91 points), Finland (89), and Sweden (89) held the top positions. Transparency International also places New Zealand (91 points) in the group of front-runners."

The Corruption Perceptions Index (CPI) 2017 (selection):[43]

Rank	Country	Rating
1	New Zealand	89
1	Denmark	88
3	Finland	85
3	Norway	85
3	Switzerland	85
6	Singapore	84
6	Sweden	84
8	Canada	82
8	Luxembourg	82
8	The Netherlands	82
8	United Kingdom	81
12	Germany	81
13	Australia	77
13	Hong Kong	77
13	Iceland	77
179	South Sudan	12
180	Somalia	9

(Rating method: 0 points are indicative of a completely corrupt situation; while 100 points indicate an absence of corruption.)

I. The Antisocial Market Economy 49

Mind you, this index does not measure corruption. Rather, it measures how corruption in the public sphere (not in the realm of private commerce) is perceived by those in power, in public administration, and by those in positions of responsibility in the economy of a country.

The Bribe Payers Index (BPI)

Turning to other rankings by Transparency International: the Bribe Payers Index, BPI, most recently from 2011, measures the preparedness of the private sector abroad to be involved in bribery. According to Transparency International's website, the BPI "ranks the likelihood of companies from [28] leading export countries and territories to bribe abroad" when conducting business.[44] The countries presented in the BPI are listed by their average value arising from the answers to those asked in the following research question: 'How often do companies which have their headquarters in (name of the country) pay bribes in this country?' The answer is given by means of a five-point scale, whereby 1 stands for "never" and 5 stands for "always."[45]

In the top spots one finds the Netherlands and Switzerland (8.8 points), Belgium (8.7), Germany, and Japan (8.6). Out of the 28 places, China and Russia take up the last two spots with 6.5 und 6.1 points, respectively. Austria was not included in the study. It should be borne in mind that this index says nothing about the situation of the willingness for corruption in the *domestic* private business sector but rather as far as international business is concerned.

The transparency ranking of multinationals

The next index prepared by Transparency International is the transparency ranking of multinationals. For this index it is not the countries of the earth but rather the 105 largest stock exchange-listed multinational companies which are investigated and put into order. The valuation is based upon publicly accessible information belonging to the respective companies, whereby transparency is seen as a precondition for the companies' successful anti-corruption policy. As a result, 0 points stands for "most non-transparent" and 10 points for "most transparent." Transparency International summarizes the results in the following manner:

> "The results are checkered. On average, transparency is above all slight when it comes to profits and the payment of taxes in countries where business is conducted. These are often the poorest countries with ques-

tionable government structures. In the case of most multinational corporations, what is least satisfactory is the reporting they do on their anti-corruption programs. Over one-half of the companies do not publish whether and how much in payments are made to political parties and politicians. Only 45 companies report exhaustively on their subsidiaries. The financial sector shows itself [...] to be especially non-transparent. Overall, the 24 multinational banks and insurance companies reported on are under average, with an average point value of 4.2 points[...]."

"The seven German companies are all found in the first third of the ranking list. What is positive is that they all report completely on their subsidiaries [...]. Not one of the seven companies from Germany publish how much in taxes their subsidiaries pay in the respective countries in which the companies are active."[46]

The Global Corruption Barometer (GCB)

The rather new Global Corruption Barometer, or GCB, is the most interesting when it comes to the actual degree of corruption in a country, and it is the most complex index compiled by Transparency International. We are again following the description on the Transparency International website.

"The Global Corruption Barometer attempts to determine the ramifications of corruption in various areas of life, to learn about expectations related to corruption, and to inquire about the priorities related to fighting corruption. In contrast to the Corruption Perceptions Index (CPI), a differentiation in individual areas is undertaken. For instance, there are political, private, familial, and commercial areas. While exclusively experts and decision makers are asked in the case of the CPI, the foundation of the Global Corruption Barometer is an assessment by the average population. [...] 114,270 people in 107 countries were asked for the 2013 Global Corruption Barometer. [...]"

"On a scale from one (no corruption) to five (highly corrupt), the judicial system (2.6) and the educational system (2.7) in Germany score particularly well. The top performers – in a negative sense – are the political parties (3.8) and the private sector (3,7). On a worldwide scale, it is also the political parties which are most frequently perceived to be the most corrupt institutions. It is conspicuous that the media (3.6) in Germany scores relatively poorly."[47]

In all areas Switzerland scores better than Germany. Austria was not included in the 2013 compilation.

I. The Antisocial Market Economy

Example: Germany and Switzerland in the 2013 Global Corruption Barometer:
From 1 (no corruption) to 5 (highly corrupt)

Sector	Germany	Switzerland
Political Parties	3.8	3.3
Private Sector	3.7	3.1
Media	3.6	3.1
Public Sector	3.4	2.7
Parliament	3.4	2.8
Medical / Physician Services	3.4	2.6
Religious Institutions	3.1	2.7
Non-Government Organizations	3.0	2.5
Military	2.9	2.6
Education System	2.7	2.2
Police	2.7	2.3
Judicial System	2.6	2.2

Now briefly some criticism from our point of view, which is that the index only reports on minor corruption but says little about large-scale corruption or the monetary extent of corruption. A number of researchers say that minor and large-scale corruption are closely linked and are in most cases correlated to each other. Wherever there is a lot of small corruption, there is always a lot of large-scale corruption. The reverse case, however, is also conceivable, and that is that there could be a relatively small amount of minor corruption while behind the scenes there is a lot of large-scale corruption. Circumstances point to the fact that repeatedly in countries belonging to the highest rated group, such as Finland, there are cases of large-scale corruption which nonetheless come to the surface.

The Eurobarometer

In addition to the international rankings, there are additional regional studies and rankings, above all for Europe. An additional representative ranking will now be presented. It was compiled within the framework of the EU-wide Eurobarometer survey. According to the Eurobarometer (No. 397, 2014, only EU member states) for the year 2013,[48] more than one-quarter (26%) of all Europeans indicate in EU surveys that they have already been affected by corruption in everyday life. This ranges from 63%

in Spain and Greece to 57% in Cyprus and Romania, 55% in Croatia, to 14% in Austria, 9% in Finland and the Netherlands, 7% in Luxembourg, 6% in France and Germany as well as 3% in Denmark.

When asked whether they had bribed someone within the last year or had been called upon to pay a bribe, on average 4% of EU citizens answered with "yes." This ranges from seven countries such as Germany with 0-1% to Austria with 5% and then to Romania with 25% and Latvia with 29%. One primarily observes in Europe that there is a vast gulf between the old EU (15 countries), which almost all were under the average of 4%, and the many corrupt new members from Eastern Europe (13 countries), which almost all lie above the average.

II. Corruption: Consequences, Legal Situation, Countermeasures

A. The consequences of corruption

Harmful consequences

The costs of corruption have to be financed, and this occurs at the expense of others! At the same time, there is the classical victim who is aware of this additional burden.

Corruption always occurs at the expense of third parties. The losses are mostly spread out upon the shoulders of many people, and the victims do not directly notice what is happening, for instance when the damage affects tax monies or prices rise unnecessarily. Companies, which on account of the corruption of others are passed over when it comes to bids, often do not know why they were passed over.

The German Federal Criminal Police Authorities (*Bundeskriminalamt*) has written the following with respect to the rising damage due to corruption: "For the year 2012, monetary damages of around €354 million were reported. This corresponds to an increase of more than 28% when compared to the prior year. Generally speaking, statements regarding the monetary dimensions of the overall amount of damages attributable to corruption are difficult to make. This is due to a situation where as a rule the financial damages caused due to obtaining permissions or winning contracts can only be vaguely exhibited. For that reason, an overall estimation of the actual magnitude of the damages caused can only be provided in a limited manner."[49]

Citizens are really only informed via reporting – where there is a functioning freedom of the press – that he or she has been harmed by corruption.

In cases of nepotism, incapable or at least less capable administrators are often elevated into office. That can have devastating consequences. However, it is only seldom evident in large-scale scandals. Also, naturally, a comparison to what serious and experienced specialists would have achieved or prevented in office is almost always absent.

Sometimes one cannot at all say whether and where damage has occurred. We will never know if the failure to elect Rainer Barzel to the office of Chancellor of what was at the time West Germany due to the German Democratic Republic's (*Deutsche Demokratische Republik*, or DDR) bribing Parliament (*Bundestag*) members was harmful or something which was beneficial, especially because the assessment one makes primarily depends on one's party preferences.

As was said at the beginning, international managers assume that on average corruption increases project costs by 10%. However, that amount could reach 25%.

Fictitious examples of unrecognized consequences: If, for instance, a municipality purchases an overpriced, lower quality fire truck, that decision has consequences for everyone and could have unnecessary and extensive material damage as a consequence. If for that reason a house burned down which would have been saved with better equipment, the owner of the house would not suspect that corruption was a possible cause. If, due to bribes, a journalist wholeheartedly recommended a less effective medication, there would possibly be many patients who would suffer due to this without knowing it or even suspecting that they had become the victims of corruption.

An example from India – sports facilities: In connection with the 2010 Commonwealth Games in New Delhi, India, billions of US dollars of the building costs for the sports facilities were misappropriated, above all through the use of inferior building materials. It is for this reason that 50 people were severely injured when a pedestrian bridge and stadium roof collapsed at the Jawaharlal-Nehru Stadium.

Fictitious example of an infrastructure project: Let us imagine that a government leader awards a USD 100 million contract for an infrastructure project that is actually superfluous. The contract is awarded because the head of government receives a bribe of 10% of the contract amount for himself or for his political party. We have taken a look at such projects. The damages reach far beyond the pure monetary sums. There are sensible or even essential projects amounting to USD 100 million where either the associated construction will not take place or another type work comprising a project will not be conducted. The funds are simply lacking for efforts to provide various supplies, education, hygiene, and security. Especially at this point, corruption keeps people in power who inflict damage on everyone, and companies are given enormous power which for the most part otherwise would not be in a position to remain in the market – or at least would not be as large and as influential.

II. Corruption: Consequences, Legal Situation, Countermeasures

Possible damages caused by corruption:
- A danger to companies which are not corrupt and to people, for example through job cuts at competing companies
- Above all a danger to smaller competitors
- Increased costs for goods and services
- Poor quality goods and services (e.g., increased repair expenses, damages due to bad quality and technological maintenance)
- Ratcheting effect: the more payoffs are made, the more competitors "have to" participate in making payoffs
- A growing gap between the rich and the poor, redistribution from the bottom to the top
- Health risks, including risks to water, food, the environment, healthcare, support services
- A lack of state finances for central efforts of the state through reduced tax revenues
- Increased costs of administration
- Promotion of the wrong abilities of government employees – instead of education, performance, and efforts it is "shrewdness" which counts
- A loss of citizens' trust in politics, administration, and the economy
- A loss of trust that leads to "I might as well do it, too"
- Democracy fails to operate
- Can lead to violent revolutions
- Economic damages
- Enables human trafficking
- Enables and promotes organized crime
- Discourages investors
- Progress and development are steered in the wrong direction because unnecessary investments prevent important investments and helpful changes
- Weakens the constitutional state and everything which the constitutional state regulates
- Violates human rights which have to do with the equality of all people
- Often cements the oppression of women
- In time it also demonstrably reduces the moral threshold for other offenses

An example from the USA - dealerships: In 1996, Honda dealers in the USA went public and stated that they were unable to buy Hondas without paying kickbacks to Honda headquarter employees. A massive case finally led to Honda's paying USD 15 million in damages to 1,800 Honda dealers for the time period 1970 to 1992. Additional dealers, who went bankrupt because they could not receive Hondas or could only receive models which were difficult to sell, won cases calling for damages.

An example from India - federal states: In India the level of corruption in the individual states varies greatly, from very low values in Kerala in the south (240 points out a possible 800 possible points) all the way to extreme values in Bihar in the north on the border to Nepal (695 points). It is easy to demonstrate that foreign investments in the individual states are higher the lower the level of corruption is.[50] It can be that there are individual corrupt firms which take advantage of the susceptibility to corruption. However, the large majority of firms are scared off.

An example from Cologne, Germany: The cartel in Cologne which has to do with awarding contracts in the public sector is expressed by means of the term "business breakfast club" because leading members of the municipal administration have regularly met in the past and still meet for breakfast with, for example, building contractors. The German word "Klüngel" (clique) is derived from "clungilin" and means a "small tangle," which thus indicates a jumble of threads hanging together which cannot be figured out. The tradition of the Cologne "Klüngel," i.e., the fusion of top offices within the city government with large Cologne businesses, reaches back into the Middle Ages. Konrad Adenauer, as the Mayor of Cologne, received large loans from the city treasury when he speculated in the stock market on the basis of insider tips without this being seen as wrong by those involved. Insider speculation on the development of share prices was not yet punishable.[51]

An example from Cologne, Germany - the Cologne garbage fees: The "garbage donations scandal" (*Müllspendenaffäre*) had to do with donations to the ruling Social Democratic Party (*Sozialdemokratische Partei Deutschland*, or SPD) which were not reported and amounted to at least 480,000 Deutschemarks between 1994 and 1999 so that the party would consent to the construction of the disputed Köln-Niehl Waste Incineration Plant (*Müllverbrennungsanlage Köln-Niehl*, or MVA). Due to laws relating to political parties, the fine the SPD was hit with amounted to twice that amount, and the SPD politicians Klaus Heugel and Norbert Rüther were sentenced to suspended sentences of close to two years in prison. In 2004, Ulrich Eisermann, the Managing Director of AVG Köln, was sentenced to almost 4 years of imprisonment. The central business figure, Hellmut Trienekens, was given a two-year suspended sentence. According to statements made by Eisermann, Cologne politicians made the financial support of party colleagues a condition of their agreement to the construction of the MVA Köln-Niehl. It was reported that fellow party member Stephan Gatter was "accommodated" and ultimately became the Chairman of the Works Council. The parliamentary party leader for the CDU, Albert Schröder, called for financial support to be provided to councilman Egbert Bischoff. The construction of the MVA Köln-Niehl cost 820 million Deutschemarks, of which 30 million Deutschemarks in kickbacks were made, all at taxpayers' expense. Furthermore, the waste incineration plant built was also much larger than permitted and necessary, for which reason it had to import waste from all over Germany and Europe. The prices outside of Cologne are significantly lower than the prices politically and contractually agreed upon for Cologne itself. As a result, residents of Cologne help to finance the waste disposal of other municipalities through their waste disposal fees.

Does the Gross Domestic Product (GDP, in German, *Bruttoinlandsprodukt*, or BIP) actually increase as a result of a reduced amount of corruption? Johann Graf Lambsdorff has written: "Analysis has shown the following: A lack of corruption has a positive effect on the relationship of GDP to the capital stock and thus increases productivity . . . If corruption in Germany would sink to the level in Denmark, which is to say that the Consumer Price Index, or CPI would rise by about 1.5%, then the income of Germans would rise by 6% on average."[52] Similar statements on the relationship of economic growth and a low level of corruption can be found more frequently. Admittedly, such statements are disputed. On the one hand, they are disputed because there are corrupt countries with strong economic growth (e.g., China, Korea). On the other hand, they are disputed because it is deemed almost impossible to calculate this effect. For that reason, we dispense with any final determination regarding this question.

It is repeatedly discussed in academia whether corruption could also not have a positive effect. So-called functionalism takes the view that corruption often promotes development because it removes obstacles to development, can ease the ascent from the bottom to the top, and better distributes resources. Naturally, this then only applies to underdeveloped and to more or less dictatorial countries.

In the meantime, it has been generally recognized that in the best case there are individual situations where the existence of corruption has brought about something better than without it, but that the overall and long-term effect is that corruption is always devastating. Excessive bureaucracy is not overcome through graft. Instead, frequent graft just brings about more dependency upon bureaucracy.

Consequences for human rights

An entire book could be filled documenting how often there is little sense in taking steps against human rights infringements if one does not simultaneously proceed against corruption. We have already addressed this topic in the introduction and in the chapter entitled "What is Corruption and who is affected by it?" in the section on "The Poorest of the Poor as Victims."

For instance, freedom of religion can be infringed upon when churches and other religious buildings are not allowed to be constructed, except when one bribes the decision makers. The right to a fair trial is obsolete if the justice system is corrupt. If corruption could be completely eradicated, then human trafficking together with forced prostitution would immediately be largely eradicated, along with a large part of organized crime. Without corruption, the poorest of the poor in many countries would have much more or even enough to live on. The right to drinking water can be endangered if through corruption water only lands in front of certain people or if the poor do not have money to pay the bribes to get to it.[53]

B. The legal foundation

The legal foundation in Germany

If one considers that in Germany bribery of (foreign) companies and individuals was not only tolerated in the 1934 Income Tax Law but even completely deductible, a lot has happened since then. In 1996, the deductibility of bribe money as a business expense was abolished, but only in cases where bribery was punishable. Only after many discussions and after pressure put on by the Organization for Economic Cooperation and Development (OECD), along with increasingly strict legislation in the USA beginning in 1977, that any related tax relief for bribery payments made domestically and abroad was completely struck from the books and has been punishable since 2002.

Both active and passive corruption, or rather, accepting and granting advantages (bribes), are addressed with respect to two areas in the German Penal Code (deutsches Strafgesetzbuch, or StGB). Those areas are politics and public administration, on the one hand, and the private sector, on the other hand. According to the German Penal Code, it is, however, only possible in both cases to bring charges against individuals (natural persons) for their corrupt behavior. A repeated call for criminal law applied to corporate corruption has not become a reality up to this day, above all due to the fact that a large part of today's legal system still rests upon 80 year-old pillars. This has also led to a situation where individuals only are convicted of crimes in clearly known incidences of bribery in international companies. Legal persons (i.e., companies) can only be sued through the path of the Code of Administrative Offences (*Gesetz über Ordnungswidrigkeiten*, or OWiG). According to § 30 of the Code of Administrative Offences, companies can also be charged fines. A well-known difficulty in the case of bribery scandals is, however, the person who gave the orders. Most often this person is not detected and is pulling the strings in the background. The individual offering the bribe, i.e., the individual handing over the money, is most of the time located significantly lower in the hierarchy and is not the main culprit.

> **Sections of the German penal code (*deutsches Strafgesetzbuch*, or StGB) against bribery, corruptibility, and granting and receiving advantages:**
> - §§ 331 ff. StGB, if office holders are involved
> - §§ 298 ff. StGB in commercial practice
> - § 108b StGB in the case of bribing voters
> - § 108e StGB in the case of bribing members of parliament
> - In addition to this, the Act Against International Corruption (*Gesetz zur Bekämpfung internationaler Bestechung*, or IntBestG) and the EU Anti-Corruption Act (*EU-Bestechungsgesetz*, [German title], or EUBestG) apply.

The specific sections in the German Penal Code are very thorough and vastly more concrete than those in the law books of most European countries. They are systematically classified under Section 26, i.e., criminal acts against competition. § 299 has to do with *passive and active corruption in commercial practice*. This has to do with accepting benefits and granting advantages within the framework of corporate activities. With this, both domestic and international cases are covered. § 300 StGB expands the preceding paragraphs by including particularly severe cases of passive and active corruption and enabling prosecution of entire networks (gangs). Often these paragraphs are cited together with additional offenses. In the case of bribery, the criminal action always calls in a favor or accepts advantages for oneself or for a third party ordering the action. The advantages mentioned can be all benefits which, for example, objectively improve the economic (or legal) situation of an individual involved.

This can have to do with payments of money, but it can also be in the form of loans, trips, or visits to bordellos. Clearly defined upper limit values for what are mere gifts and where bribery begins are things which are not, however, found in the law (indeed there are such guidelines for administrative procedures, for instance for federal employees), and in actual fact the limits for public office holders is set much lower than in the private business sector.

The largest German scandals have mostly been tied to § 266 StGB and its definition of breach of trust in addition to pure bribery. The affair surrounding Siemens and Flick mostly began through uncovering slush funds which had been established and which allowed a system of corruption to be financed domestically and internationally. Through this, there were individual perpetrators who were able to be brought to account for having channeled off funds from accounts of their trustors in order to run these illegal tills. This was done either in special accounts or in the form of cash. In contrast to the paragraphs on bribery, there is no presupposed *effort for self-enrichment* on the part of the perpetrator. It is the act in itself which is punishable.

The bribery of public officials falls under § 331-335 of the German Penal Code (StGB). The term "office holder" is understood very broadly and includes individuals in elected offices, civil servants, members of public services, but also those who have public service obligations and members of the armed forces. The term refers to elected offices according to international terms of reference such as the Anti-Corruption Commission of the European Council, the Council of Europe's Group of States against Corruption, or GRECO, and the UN Convention against Corruption (UN-CAC), which seeks to define numerous terms with international consistency. Many parts of the German Penal Code are thus UN law, which is codified in Germany via the circuitous EU route. The definition of *public official* also comes under this definition. This is translated as an *office holder* in German, and there are many actions which are criminally legally actionable with respect to them, including bribery. Imprisonment for accepting or granting undue advantage seems to be part of the general consensus in a large part of the Western European economic area.

According to § 331 StGB, in the corruption of office holders, as well as when it comes to members of commercial businesses, there is a distinction made between *active and passive corruption*. Yet this is of no significant relevance when it comes to punishment. The party bribed, in particular as a member of an agency or as a member of the German Army, can be punished with up to five years of imprisonment (§ 334 StGB). The same applies to the party offering the bribe.

II. Corruption: Consequences, Legal Situation, Countermeasures

There greatest point of weakness in Germany's battle against corruption is supposedly the lack of a state guarantee of protection for whistleblowers and an obligation for companies to guarantee such employees a point of contact.

Whistleblower example – from the private sector: In 2011, it was decided for the first time by the European Court of Human Rights that it was unjustified to terminate a geriatric nurse for having filed charges owing to the severe deficiencies in her employer's care facilities. It is not understandable how German courts had decided otherwise prior to that time.

Whistleblower example – from public administration: Up to the year 2005, the Münster tax investigator Werner Borcharding had fought to take up his place again in his old position: he had correctly filed charges against the Regional Finance Office (*Oberfinanzdirektion*) and its bosses because these individuals had purposely covered up the tax evasion of a local industrial company. His letters to the then Finance Minister Peer Steinbrück and other authorities had remained unanswered. At the age of 57, the civil servant went into early retirement.

These and similar cases show that state whistleblower protection is urgently necessary. Especially employees are not protected from being terminated by their employer, and in agencies the unwelcome employees are often forced into positions where they can no longer cause difficulties on account of "the impairment of the freedom of holding office" (included in the opinion of the Administrative Court of Münster' in Borcharding's case). Regarding the tax evasion case of the chairman of FC Bayern (Bavarian professional soccer team), Ulli Hoeneß, the German newspaper Frankfurter Allgemeine Zeitung (FAZ) wrote the following: "It is conspicuous that statements made by an informant, who had repeatedly gone via a renowned lawyer for whistleblowers to register additional accusations with the authorities, shipwrecked when it came to dealing with the Munich Ministry of Justice. The Munich Ministry of Justice refused to offer him the requested informant protection."[54]

Despite many similar cases, the ratification of the UN Convention against Corruption does not appear in the new German Federal Government Coalition Agreement, although this had beforehand been stridently called for by representatives of the government and opposition. Also, the commitment agreed upon in Seoul at the G20 Summit to legally anchor the protection of whistleblowers by 2012, was not implemented. Therefore, one can speak of bipartisan rejection of protection of *informers*, as individuals providing information in politics are repeatedly and disparagingly referred to.

Since a 2003 judgment by the District Court of Cologne, council members of a municipality count as administrative office holders and not as parliamentarians. This was a great step forward in the battle against municipal corruption.

The legal situation in Austria

It was already in 1964 that Austria passed its first anti-corruption law. However, the law exclusively related to the bribery of domestic civil servants and, more specifically, the heads of public companies. The expansion to include the private economic sector did not occur until over 40 years later. While in 2008 GRECO still criticized over 24 points of Austrian legal practice with respect to combating corruption – a magnitude otherwise known among Eastern European candidates for EU accession – this deficit has been taken into account since that time, specifically in the area of criminal law and in the area of abuse of office. Particularly the Criminal Law Amendment Act of 2008 (*Strafrechtsänderungsgesetz 2008*, or StRÄG 2008) brought about a number of improvements for what is presently the Penal Code's (*Strafgesetzbuches*, or StGB) §§ 304-310, for instance the introduction of the term for an office holder. Office holders are defined as "civil servants as well as contracted officials as well as every person who performs public duties." According to § 304, receiving or granting advantages in connection with the administration of one's duties is punishable by up to three years of imprisonment.

That touched off a lot of controversy in Austria since these terms were not known before. There were in part public discussions about whether a bouquet of flowers for a teacher was to be taken as a form of bribery. What was overlooked in the process is that Austria just largely implemented guidelines which had already been adopted by the EU Parliament, had long been codified in other countries, and which predominantly rested upon demands of the United Nations Convention against Corruption.

Furthermore, through the introduction of the element of the offense of *sweetening up*, the possibility was also created of punishing granting advantages where there was a wide separation of time between the granting of advantages and the time when official duties were conducted. Prior thereto, this had only been possible with great effort. The terms for office holder and sweetening up were again made more precise in the Corruption Criminal Law Amendment Act of 2009 (*Korruptionsstrafrechtsänderungsgesetz*, or KorrStrÄG). Nevertheless, the punishment for active corruption is significantly less punished and, more specifically, the attempt alone is not yet punishable. Passive corruption is, however, punishable in any event. This includes a mere promise or notification. In § 168 of the StGB, corruption in the private sector is regulated, whereby individuals who can be bribed are broadly defined as "officials" and "commissioners" of an institution established under private law.

In Austria, there are at least initial tendencies towards the Ministry of Justice's installing a form of protection for whistleblowers through, among others, a whistleblower service on the internet. However, this is still designed without state guaranteed protection and is thus largely useless in practice. The responsibility for transparency relating to party finances still leaves much to be desired.

The legal situation in Switzerland

Since the 1990s, anti-corruption laws have been consistently applied, as international organizations repeatedly attest. Switzerland lies, so to speak, in line with the international trend in combating corruption. As an OECD member, Switzerland has ratified the OECD conventions against bribing office holders as well as the United Nations Convention against Corruption, whereby the former significantly changed the Swiss penal code. In accordance with this, bribery is broken down into three essential types: bribery of office holders, bribery between private individuals and the penal consequences for business. The former, as in Germany and Austria, is based upon the principle of the incorruptibility of office holders and is regulated in Article 322 of the Swiss Penal Code by breaking actions down into active and passive bribery. The important term of *sweetening up* is also defined here. Penalties in Germany and Switzerland can reach up to 5 years of imprisonment. Bribing private individuals is also found in the national Unfair Commercial Practices Law (*Bundesgesetz gegen den unlauteren Wettbewerb*). The most severe penalty here is 3 years of imprisonment. Companies themselves can be directly punished according to Article 102, provided that a natural person cannot be held accountable.

In Switzerland, corruption among non-governmental agents (companies, banks, association) is generally not prosecuted. According to the laws as they stand, something can only be undertaken upon request. It is astonishing that Switzerland, despite this lack of prosecution of private corruption, comes out better in all the rankings than Germany. It is also astonishing that despite its direct form of democracy, Switzerland does not have disclosure requirements when it comes to political party donations. As a result, it is unknown which banks, companies, and individuals support which parties. There is also no state guarantee protecting whistleblowers in Switzerland, as well as no corresponding guarantee of protection for employees.

Perpetrators' justification strategies[55]

- Denying illegality: ("What was done was within my space to maneuver." "That was after all my own decision to make.")
- Denial of responsibility ("There was no other way of doing it." "It didn't hurt anyone." "Anyone in my position would have done that.")
- Pointing to the partner's responsibility ("He should have known that." "They forced me to do it.")
- Pointing to the environment ("Otherwise someone else would have done it." "Everyone does it.")
- Denying that there are victims or that it causes damage ("It didn't hurt anyone. That is just the way it is in a free enterprise economy – there are always some losers.")
- Pointing to a win-win situation ("It was a good deal for both sides.")
- Pointing to the positive benefit, for example safeguarding jobs ("It was the only way to save the company.")
- Redirecting attention ("Others are doing it even more frequently." "Our laws are so confusing anyway.")
- Pressure to adapt: common commercial practice ("My bosses expect that . . ." "No one cares how I make a profit as long as I make one").
- Individual, self-set limits ("It was only a matter of small amounts.")
- Pointing to the benefit of others (e.g., for the political party): ("It wasn't even for me.")
- Self-justification ("It is my right." "I've earned it after so many years." "If they had paid me better . . .")
- Blurring the situation ("It is something I just do on the side." "My special knowledge is simply being rewarded." "It is just a gift from friends from the past.")

C. Governance

Good governance

Progress is not only a question of economic growth. Rather, it is also a question of so-called *good governance*. *Governance* here comprises much more than only what a government does. Namely, it includes everything that has to do with leading, administering, and improving the state and society. The same applies to responsible state governance. The term governance has been a technical term used by historians and political scientists. Use of the word *good* came about in the 1980s and was developed into an alternative concept by the World Bank, the UN's development program, and by the OECD's development program through experience with *bad* governance.

Above all, there was a report by the World Bank in 1989 which viewed the cause of the crisis in Africa to be bad governance. This use of the expression ensured that the term *governance* ascended to become a key term in the international discussion on development after the collapse of the communist empire.

The World Bank held the following to be the mistakes and causes of the poverty and growth catastrophes of African countries:

Five elements of bad governance according to the World Bank – 1989:
- Unreliable legal system
- Weak public management
- Insufficient tie between the actions of government and the administrative handling of legislation
- Lack of transparency with respect to administration and the use of funds
- Thinking in terms of benefits on the part of the elite, which leads to rampant corruption

---

As a counterpart, principles of good government were developed over time. In 2007 and 2009, for example, Article 41 of the Charter of Fundamental Rights of the European Union anchored the fundamental right to *good administration*. Despite this, what still applies is that every individual understands something different by the term *good governance*.

> *Elements of good governance:*
> - The rule of law, linking public action to legislation
> - Transparent and efficient public financial systems
> - Functioning, just, and transparent administration
> - Fighting corruption and the personal enrichment of ruling individuals
>
> *Reasons for rampant corruption in developing countries:*
> - Corrupt heads of state
> - Stronger link to, for example, the extended family, clan, ethnic group, or religious community than to the state and law
> - Lack of or disintegrating infrastructure
> - Poorly equipped and/or poorly functioning administration
> - Poorly paid office holders and civil servants
> - A culture of providing gifts to office holders
> - Corrupt prosecution and judiciary preventing the battle against corruption

Good governance and democracy

Democracy means more than just free elections. In reality, free elections are the best means to a higher purpose – freedom, justice, and the protection of human rights for everyone. The rights of minorities stand superior to, for example, majority votes by parliament.

But for all that, the impression is repeatedly awakened as if the act of electing in itself brings about *good governance* and democracy in this narrow sense and that democracy in this narrow sense also prevents corruption. In actual fact, however, the development of the Commonwealth of Independent States (CIS) and Eastern European states demonstrates that half-democracies as well as functioning democracies cannot prevent corruption from taking the upper hand. What happens in democracies is that political corruption often is distributed upon the shoulders of many. This is due to the fact that in only a few democracies is there one individual who has, for example, power equivalent to that of the President of the United States of America. With that said, the number of individuals who tend to have the potential for political corruption grows.

For example, the fact that elections themselves are no panacea against corruption is seen in Turkey. Although it is apparent that Recep Tayyip Erdogan and his political companions are enriching themselves enormously and are sanctioning corruption from the top down, indeed having transferred or dismissed thousands of investigating civil servants, Erdogan is again and again voted into office by large majorities. A similar example is Silvio Berlusconi in Italy, who was entangled in corruption to a great extent. Indeed, he had intertwined business and politics completely and had protected himself with immunity and laws passed only for his protection ("lex Berlusconi"). In completely free elections he was repeatedly voted in as Prime Minister and can count on a significant portion of the voting public up to this day. The South African President Jacob Zuma hardly takes any trouble to cover up his corruption and muzzles his critics. Despite this, he can nonetheless depend on a healthy majority of voters.

Please do not understand this as a criticism of democracy. However, when a democracy does not realize how susceptible it is to corruption and does not ensure that the separation of powers, which assumes that power corrupts, be truly taken seriously and that the large parties have an equal say in all matters, they can fall behind countries which are not democratic or are half-democratic with respect to corruption. Let us take as an example a comparison between Jamaica and Singapore:[56]

Fifty years ago, Singapore and Jamaica were approximately the same size with respect to population, with 1.8 million people, and were similarly poor. At that time, most Jamaicans had more opportunities than Singaporeans. The per capita gross national product of Singapore has grown six-fold, while that of Jamaica grew 25% in the first ten years and has been stagnant for 40 years. Today per capita gross national product is even somewhat lower than the 1972 level. The mortality rate up to the fifth year of life is eight times higher in Jamaica than in Singapore. Singapore has the lowest murder rate in the world, while Jamaica's murder rate is very high and has climbed fivefold since 1972.

What is alarming is the following: Jamaica is a democracy with two parties which alternate at the pinnacle of power approximately every 10 years. However, it is a poorly managed country with a lot of corruption, democracy or no democracy. Singapore, on the other hand, has comparatively free elections by which the same party, however, has been elected by a large majority since 1959. It rules the country rather autocratically There are closely meshed laws and detailed controls. However, the all-dominant party has ensured that there is an extremely well-functioning administration, radical anti-corruption measures, and a high level of domestic security. Although corruption was part of everyday culture in the 1960s, in the meantime this has largely dried up.

Democracy with a high level of corruption can be more damaging and more unjust than a half-democracy with a just administration and judiciary coupled with very low corruption, because a democracy with a high level of corruption hardly is a democracy.

D. Battling corruption

Possible measures

In the following, a number of suggestions for fighting corruption will be given. However, they cannot be taken as a substitute for specialist publications or serve as a guide for specific authorities or for a company.

One can – for instance in following the Austrian Federal Bureau of Anti-Corruption (*Bundesamt zur Korruptionsprävention und Korruptionsbekämpfung*, or BAK) – distinguish between several phases of battling corruption:[57]

1) (prior) Prevention: analysis of acts of corruption and prevention measures which develop from them at every level, theoretically as well as practically
2) (prior) Education / schooling / awareness raising
3) (during) Repression, externally through authorities and inspectors as well as internally
4) (after) Control, and punishment as necessary, externally as well as internally.

Actually, one should organically plan for anti-corruption measures and include them from the very beginning when it comes to founding every agency and every company and when starting any project.

Thus there are important rules of thumb which need to be incorporated into the system. For instance, rules of thumb are needed that unconditionally control visual inspection of documents and contain results (e.g., of purchased assets, of buildings and local events). Additionally, it should never be the case that only one person is responsible from beginning to end for procurement or for a project. Experience teaches just the opposite, that rotation and regrouping senior employees is not always the solution. Through these measures, corruption can also just gradually spread throughout an entire system.

Anti-corruption officers: Anti-corruption officers have been tried and tested (especially in agencies but also in companies and NGOs). However, they should be experienced auditors and know the actual running of

II. Corruption: Consequences, Legal Situation, Countermeasures 69

their businesses from the inside, along with all its secrets, i.e., they should not be chosen on the basis of political viewpoints or on criteria foreign to performance.

Central allocation office: What has likewise been tried and tested for agencies and companies is a "central allocation office." Planning takes place at demand offices, but tenders and procurement take place separately in a central office which has to guarantee freedom from corruption.

Code of ethics: A code of ethics should be available in written form, should be understandable, and should mention good reasons which likewise apply for everyone from the greatest to the smallest, name disciplinary consequences, indicate who are the points of contact, and mention the mediation committees. Additionally, it should be a living document which is communicated clearly and is repeatedly the object of discussions at all levels.

Integrity pact: What is recommendable in the case of larger projects is to have foundational agreements for all participants, even if they do not all conduct business with each other. "The integrity pact is an instrument which was developed by Transparency International and is a globally applied instrument to which primarily the contracting entity and all suppliers and contractors submit themselves to, with clear compliance regulations and likewise clear threats of sanctions."[58] This form of integrity pact has stood the test internationally and is being used in Germany in connection with the construction of the international airport in Berlin-Brandenburg.

Guidelines: The International Chamber of Commerce published a comprehensive report on corruption in business for the first time in 1977 and in the process expressed recommendations for action. Since 2008 there are, in addition, special guidelines which were most recently revised in 2011.[59]

Freedom of the press: Freedom of the press is very important for combating corruption. It is not by chance that corrupt rulers such as the Turkish Prime Minister Erdogan or the Russian President Putin have limited the freedom of the press or even the use of Facebook and Twitter.

What is always important is that the risk of discovery is very high, for it is often this risk which decides whether corruption takes place or not.

In all this, one should not forget, however, that all measures only have a purpose if in the end there is a state standing there which wants to end corruption. Every effective battle against corruption has to bump up against a sensible and applied penal code, the consequent application of which in turn rises and falls with the independence and material, personnel-based, and professional layout of the public prosecutors. Next, the state has to lead the way by example. This is due to the fact that the top performers of all rankings put out by Transparency International are countries with a strong level of transparency within politics and administration, resting upon comprehensive laws guaranteeing freedom of information and inviting all citizens to play a part.

Whistleblowers[60]

Experience demonstrates that corruption (and other economic crime) is seldom uncovered by internal or external audits. Much more frequently it comes from whistleblowers and/or coincidences. All of the most recent cases in Germany such as Daimler, VW, Siemens, Ikea, or Allianz are traceable back to courageous whistleblowers. It can thus happen that individuals professionally dealing with control have to become whistleblowers since their superiors block the forwarding or realization of results, as we will see further below in the text dealing with the example of Paul van Buitenens.

According to a 2009 study of German companies by PricewaterhouseCoopers, 41% of discovered cases of economic crime were traceable back to internal whistleblowers and 21% to external whistleblowers.

The German Federal Criminal Police Office has written: "Corruption is a crime of control. Successes in the battle against the crime of corruption depend strongly upon producing qualified pieces of evidence. Around two-thirds of the proceedings were initiated by corresponding external tips, and the compliance structures which had been established in many companies might have even contributed to these tips. The further expansion of these structures could lead to a further qualitative and quantitative increase in incoming tips in the future."[61]

Whistleblowers are mostly either truly incorruptible with respect to tips, or no longer wishing to put up with the abuse, or they finally have found evidence, or they are corrupt individuals who want to get out because it has become too dangerous for them, or they are no longer being taken care of attentively, or they have no more influence to offer which can be converted into money. Corrupt relationships can last for years and decades, but they are often nevertheless very precarious, for instance if the partnership is no longer profitable, if it is not being sufficiently cultivated, if a partner is always wanting more, or if the partnership is in an environment where controlling authorities are getting closer and each individual is seeking to save his own skin.

II. Corruption: Consequences, Legal Situation, Countermeasures 71

Whistleblower-net has commissioned several studies and has conducted studies. "One important finding in these studies is that up to now in Germany the great potential employees and organizations/companies have in a commonly designed and responsible and transparently driven whistleblower system has mostly not been put to use. Most systems are prescribed from above without their users being taken along and enthused for the idea. Many systems load down employees in a one-sided manner with what are in part legally highly questionable reporting requirements and leave it to top management to decide what happens with the reports."[62]

Germany, Austria, and Switzerland lack laws protecting such whistleblowers against labor law and even service law reprisals.

> *Classical countermeasures or punishments by corrupt companies against whistleblowers:*
> - Additional corruption, i.e., an offer, for example, of money or a promotion in order to keep quiet
> - Threats on account of non-compliance with labor law requirements, confidentiality obligations, and prescribed chains of command
> - Reprimands
> - Claims for damages
> - Aggressive bossing, bullying, ostracism
> - Loss of in-house status, termination
> - Reprimands against supporters and witnesses
> - Poor chances of finding new work after dismissal, warnings provided to potential new employers

Even judges often expect that whistleblowers will initially try to clear up the matter within the company. Why on earth? When it has to do with offenses relevant to tax and criminal proceedings? Is it imperative that a family member who is severely mistreated also first go and involve a family therapist before he or she goes to the police?

According to a 2009 study by PricewaterhouseCoopers of German companies, only a third of German firms have any sort of anti-corruption program at all. According to a further study dating from 2010, only a quarter of the surveyed state authorities had such a program. Whistleblowers are naturally not in good hands and are better served if they immediately turn to outside bodies, above all when they do not know who among their superiors or among their points of contact in the company are entangled in corruption.

Paul van Buitenen

Through his incorruptibility and on account of an unbelievable chain of corruption, Paul van Buitenen, a convinced Christian – acting completely in the vein of Old Testament prophets – led to the resignation of the EU Commission in 1999.[63] As a result, he lost his job with the EU. He is a textbook example of what can even happen to whistleblowers in committees such as the EU Commission, who themselves incessantly speak about combating corruption and force others to take measures to fight corruption. Furthermore, he is an example of how civil servants responsible for compliance can become whistleblowers.

As a compliance officer for the EU Commission, Van Buitenen found irrefutable evidence of illegal allocation of aid money from the Leonardo da Vinci VET Programme which was supposed to be targeted for continuing education.[64] The European Commission anti-corruption authorities did not pay attention to his report. His own department investigated, but then refused to investigate the directorship and prohibited von Buitenen from conducting additional investigations. However, he continued to make private notes, sent these to all superiors, and threatened to submit them to the EU Parliament. Subsequent thereto, an investigative report by his agency which appeared on July 17, 1998, confirmed all the charges. Again, however, it was not attended to. The General Director forbade van Buitenen from forwarding it to the European Court of Auditors and the EU Parliament. On December 9, 1998, van Buitenen finally sent 75 copies to the Chairman of the Green Faction asking that they be forwarded to the EU Budget Control Commission. The report also described how this and many other corruption investigations had been prevented by higher office holders all the way up to the French commissioner. After that, van Buitenen was placed on leave and his salary was halved. Later he was transferred to building management and in the end was supposed to never again work as an EU compliance officer. In actual fact, though, he should have been made the head of the anti-corruption department! When van Buitenen finally went to the press, there were a number of commissioners and the Commission as a whole who accused him of incompetence and lying. On March 15, 1999 a committee of experts delivered a scathing report commissioned by the EU Parliament which confirmed all of van Buitenen's charges. On the same evening the entire commission resigned. Van Buitenen, who is today an EU representative in the battle against corruption in the EU, is still considered a black sheep in the EU Commission. He was never truly vindicated, let alone thanked for his actions. The EU Parliament has refused up to the present day to introduce protection for whistleblowers or at least a form of protection for its own compliance officers so that something of this sort can never happen again.

Systems for providing tips

Evidence suggests that the mere existence of a system for dealing with tips can have a deterring effect, regardless of whether it is a matter of ombudsman, anonymous telephone calls, or external, trusted lawyers. Actually, in order to save money, every agency, every company, and every association should at least for economic reasons be interested to experience as quickly and as exhaustively as possible where it has been damaged!

Therefore, there are external lawyers acting as ombudsmen for the Deutsche Bahn and for the states of Rhineland-Palatinate and Hamburg who confidentially accept tips. North Rhine-Westphalia has installed a corruption hotline to a special unit of the state criminal police authorities. Schleswig-Holstein has installed an independent anti-corruption officer with whom informants can speak.

The Lower Saxony Police have established the Business Keeper Monitoring System (BKMS) internet platform, by which whistleblowers can anonymously communicate with the police. Most of the time a single tip is not enough. The platform operates in a way that allows the police to re-contact the whistleblower after a plausibility check. Through this platform, approximately 150 criminal proceedings are initiated every year. The platform can also be adopted by private companies.

A list of demands for combating corruption

The absence of preventative measures in companies against corruption was made a punishable offense in Great Britain In 2010. Such evidence that measures have been taken should also become a matter of course for authorities, large companies, and NGOs here in Germany. For there are always many people who have to pay the cost of corruption, and often enough it is directly or indirectly taxpayers who end up footing the bill.

Demands for combating corruption:
- Lengthen the statute of limitations (Corruption lapses in Germany after 5 years. Since corruption is linked to secrecy and deception and is often not discovered until much later, this period of time is much too short.)
- Strict rules for lobbyists
- Police and compliance authorities should be better equipped as far as personnel and equipment are concerned (replace antiquated computers, for example)
- Have specialized prosecutors' offices, such as in Munich and Frankfurt
- Have more judges and public prosecutors and associated employees (this would pay for itself through preventing the skimming off of excess profits)
- Limit the authority to instruct public prosecutors on how their investigations are to proceed and make the investigations transparent (permitting only accessible, justifiable written files)
- Training in order to improve the skills of prosecuting authorities
- Treat these topics during the period of education (e.g., during law school, during business administration, administrative science, and education science studies)
- Promote business ethics
- Increase research
- Prohibit nepotism and include it in the penal code
- Introduce a corporate criminal code so that corporations can be charged with crimes – such as there is in the USA, France, and Switzerland
- Include all offenses of corruption in the Money Laundering Act
- Improve the fight against skimming off excess profits – immorality should not be allowed to be pay off
- Keep a register of corruption according to the Scandinavian example
- Have better telephone monitoring of corrupt civil servants and companies
- Transparency in administration and politics
- Strict guidelines for every company and every agency
- Four-eyes principle and a system of responsibility rotation within administrative bodies
- Protection for whistleblowers
- Leniency programs
- So-called observational studies are to be forbidden in healthcare

III. Corruption – The Bible's View

A. Corruption from the viewpoint of the Bible

In the Old Testament as well as in the New Testament, God is very frequently presented under the title of the highest judge, whose absolute sense of justice and incorruptibility is the point of departure for the rejection of all perversion of justice out of the lust for money and power. That shows that the topic of corruption in the Bible and in Judeo-Christian ethics is at the top of the agenda. A society with corruption can, by definition, not be a just society. God is one "who shows no partiality and accepts no bribes,"[65] "for with the Lord our God there is no injustice or partiality or bribery."[66]

One finds the New Testament counterpart to the Old Testament witness of the incorruptibility of God in the temptation of Jesus (Matthew 4, Luke 4). At the beginning of his ministry, Jesus had to demonstrate his incorruptibility. He did not allow himself to be bribed with bread or with power. Also, Jesus did not allow himself to be led by avarice and a lust for power. Rather, when the devil promised him power over all the kingdoms of the earth – the largest bribe which was ever offered anyone – he was led by the will of God.

This demonstrates that bribery and corruption, i.e., perverting justice and bending the law by offering money, influence, and power is truly no minor peccadillo in the Bible. Rather, it is a central topic.[67] The topic of corruption shows, therefore, how little one can separate personal sin from societal sin in the Bible. There are always individuals participating in corruption, and yet corruption is an evil to which an entire network of evil structures belong and that can bring an entire society down into the abyss. This is due to the fact that it can eat up those who are responsible in all areas of the society, i.e., in the church, in commerce, and in the state political and administrative structures.

The Hebrew root (*schd*), from which the word "bribe" (Hebrew: *sochad*) stems, actually means *to ruin*. The word corruption comes from the corresponding Latin translation *corruptio*, which likewise means *to ruin* and *to destroy*. *Corruptio* is not just incidentally the Latin word for *original sin*, which designates original sin and, with that said, the fall of humankind in Catholic teaching and in the confessions of the Reformation. Adam and Eve allow themselves to be persuaded to rebel against God and his peace (*shalom*) through the offer of power and knowledge ("you will be like God," Genesis 3:5). Church tradition sees the *natura corrupta*, the corrupt heart, to be the root not only of actual corruption but rather harmful conduct towards others in general.

To accept bribes is always wrong and is condemned innumerable times in the Old Testament (e.g., Exodus 23:8; Proverbs 15:27; 17:8, Ecclesiastes 7:7; Ezekiel 22:12; Job 15:34). Corruption and bribery are always strictly forbidden in court (Deuteronomy 27:25; Proverbs 17:8 and 17:23; Isaiah 33:15; Ezekiel 22:12).

The Bible repeatedly reports against people who allow themselves to be led astray to do evil or demand payoffs or offer them. Thus, we find Judas in the New Testament, who betrayed Jesus for money (Matthew 27:3; Acts 1:18), the guards at the tomb of Jesus who made false statements for money (Matthew 28:12), the sorcerer Simon who wanted to purchase the power of the Holy Spirit from Peter (Acts 8:20), and the judge Felix, who was willing to acquit Paul if Paul would pay him money (Acts 24:26).

Perhaps there is no better text demonstrating the contemptibleness of corruption, which increasingly devours all areas of life and spoils and destructs society from the top down, than the indictment made by the prophet Micah: "Both hands are skilled in doing evil; the ruler demands gifts, the judge accepts bribes, the powerful dictate what they desire – they all conspire together."[68] Every individual at the top is using his power and follows avarice instead of justice. In the process, one hand is washing the other ("they all conspire together"). In the end it is like an octopus; one can cut off many of its arms without ever being able to truly eliminate it.

Once it reaches the point that the crossover between deceit and corruption in the various structures of authority are fluid, the people of God are not excluded, not clearly preaching against corruption and every form of avarice, even in fact letting themselves be bribed. At another point, Micah brings a charge: "Her leaders judge for a bribe, her priests teach for a price, and her prophets tell fortunes for money"[69].

It is expressly pointed out in the Old Testament, and especially by the prophets, that in the battle against corruption the precondition is the battle against exploitation of the poor![70]

B. A collision of duties in the case of small-scale corruption among predominantly poor people

The Old and the New Testaments welcome gifts. People give gifts in order to help other people or to make them happy. With all the necessary warning against corruption, a warning should not lead a necessary and healthy culture of gift-giving to by and large fall into disrepute.

The Bible is very sober and realistic, also with the fact that a collision of duties can sometimes lead to a situation where gifts are mandatory in order to achieve legitimate things which are otherwise being withheld. What is it that is said by the teacher of wisdom? "A gift given in secret soothes anger, and a bribe concealed in the cloak pacifies great wrath."[71] If a poor person encounters a civil servant who is open to bribery, and there is no present or other prospect of eradicating this corruptibility, in our opinion he can – also as a Christian – do as we did in Indonesia (see the "Introduction to the Topic") in order to effect the fulfillment of his rights through the use of gifts.

To pay bribes is also allowed to a certain degree if through it no bending of the rules takes place but rather that which is permitted and legitimate is made possible or damage by another is averted.[72] No one condemns those Jews who were able to purchase their own freedom or the freedom of others from concentration camps. Likewise, there is often nothing else the poor and powerless can do than to purchase medical treatment or a spot for a child in a school. It should be clear that this is to nevertheless occur with great caution and reservation, and that it only applies to countries and situations in which there are no other possibilities (for instance, a complaint against a boss, access to the court system, or an alternative way to achieve what is sought after).

What one is dealing with here is a classic collision of duties. It should also be clear that bribery for vanities or even for unlawful things is as unthinkable as the use of bribery in a constitutional state where there are functioning ways to proceed if an individual is denied things to which he or she is legally entitled.

A Christian who is forced to pay should also nevertheless fight against the evil of corruption, starting particularly with combating every form of openness to bribes.

An ethical conflict, or conflict of duties, emerges when two values and commands or prohibitions come into conflict. A frequent conflict in the Bible has to do with the two commands to not kill and not to lie, thus the fifth and the sixth commandments. Since the command to protect life is above the command not to lie, in the case of extreme conflict a lie can save a life. This is repeatedly justified using the example of the prostitute Rahab, although there are many other examples in the Old Testament (e.g., Exodus 1:15-21; Exodus 2:3-9; Joshua 2:1-22; Psalm 34; 1 Samuel 16:2; 19:9-17; 2 Samuel 17:18-21). Also, no one is required to give true information if it is to be used to kill (for instance, when Nazis wanted to know where Jews were hidden).

IV. Suggestions and Further Literature

Suggestions

We recommend obtaining a book specializing in combating corruption in the area having to do with your profession (for example, a guidebook on combating corruption in administration, commerce, medicine, the media, athletics, or politics) and following recommendations you find there.

Furthermore, we recommend that you ask about the corruption prevention program in every institution to which you belong, in which you exert influence, and with which you regularly have involvement. Another option would be to encourage the introduction of such a program in your local municipality, with your local authorities, in your company, your party, your church congregation, and the associations in which you are a member.

Further literature

All of the internet links cited were checked in August, 2018 to confirm that they were up to date.

Transparency International Reports

Corruption Perceptions Index 2018. Transparency International. https://www.transparency.org/cpi2018.

Corruption Perceptions Index 2017. Transparency International. https://www.transparency.org/news/feature/corruption_perceptions_index_2017.

The 2011 Bribe Payers Index. Transparency International. http://www.transparency.org/bpi2011.

Global Corruption Barometer 2017. Transparency International. https://www.transparency.org/whatwedo/publication/people_and_corruption_citizens_voices_from_around_the_world

Global Corruption Barometer 2013. Transparency International. http://www.transparency.org/gcb2013.

Transparency in Corporate Reporting 2016. Transparency International. https://www.transparency.org/whatwedo/publication/transparency_in_corporate_reporting_assessing_emerging_market_multinat.

Transparency in Corporate Reporting 2015. Transparency International. http://www.transparency.org/whatwedo/publication/transparency_in_corporate_reporting_assessing_the_worlds_largest_telecommun.

Global Corruption Report 2016: Sport. Transparency International. https://www.transparency.org/whatwedo/publication/global_corruption_report_sport

Global Corruption Report 2013: Education. Transparency International. http://www.transparency.org/whatwedo/pub/global_corruption_report_education.

Global Corruption Report 2011: Climate Change. Transparency International. http://www.transparency.org/whatwedo/publication/global_corruption_report_climate_change.

Global Corruption Report 2009: Corruption and the Private Sector. Transparency International. http://www.transparency.org/whatwedo/publication/global_corruption_report_2009.

Global Corruption Report 2007: Corruption in Judicial Systems. Transparency International. http://www.transparency.org/whatwedo/publication/global_corruption_report_2007_corruption_and_judicial_systems.

Global Corruption Report 2004: Special Focus: Political Corruption. Transparency International. http://www.transparency.org/whatwedo/publication/global_corruption_report_2004_political_corruption.

International

https://en.wikipedia.org/wiki/Corruption

Paul M. Heywood (ed.). *Routledge Handbook of Political Corruption*. Routledge: London, 2014

Laurence Cockcroft. *Global Corruption: Money, Power and Ethics in the Modern World*. London/New York: I. B. Tauris, 2012.

International Council on Human Rights. Corruption and Human Rights: Making the Connection. Transparency International, 2009. http://www.ichrp.org/files/reports/40/131_web.pdf.

Ann M. Florini, editor. *The Third Force: The Rise of Transnational Civil Society*. Carnegie Endowment for Int'l Peace, 2012.

In German:

Jahrbuch Korruption 2006: Schwerpunkt: Korruption im Gesundheitssektor. Berlin: Parthas, 2006.

Matthias S. Fifka, Andreas Falke (eds.). Korruption als internationales Phänomen. Berlin: Erich Schmidt, 2012.

Raymond Fisman, Edward Miguel. Economic Gangsters: Korruption und Kriminalität in der Weltwirtschaft. Frankfurt a. M./New York: Campus, 2009.

Markus Flückiger. Geschenk und Bestechung: Korruption im afrikanischen Kontext. Bonn: VKW, 2000.

Birger P. Priddat, Michael Schmid (eds.). Korruption als Ordnung zweiter Art. Wiesbaden: VS Verlag/Springer, 2011.

Europe – Reports

Eurobarometer – Corruption. EU: Brussels, 2017. http://ec.europa.eu/commfront office/publicopinion/index.cfm/Survey/getSurveyDetail/search/corruption/surveyKy/2176

EU Anti-Corruption Report 2014. European Commission. https://ec.europa.eu/home-affairs/sites/homeaffairs/files/e-library/documents/policies/organized-crime-and-human-trafficking/corruption/docs/acr_2014_en.pdf.

The Costs of Corruption across the EU. The GreensEFA: Brussels, 2018. https://www.greens-efa.eu/files/doc/docs/e46449daadbfebc325a0b408bbf5ab1d.pdf

Money, Politics, Power: Corruption Risks in Europe. Transparency International, 2012. http://www.transparency.org/whatwedo/publication/money_politics_and_power_corruption_risks_in_europe.

Whistleblowing in Europe: Legal protections for whistleblowers in the EU. Transparency International, 2013. http://www.transparency.org/whatwedo/publication/whistleblowing_in_europe_legal_protections_for_whistleblowers_in_the_eu.

"Corruption." Special Eurobarometer No 397, 2014. http://ec.europa.eu/public_opinion/archives/ebs/ebs_397_en.pdf.

Europe – Books

Andreas Oldag, Hans-Martin Tillack. *Spaceship Brussels – How Democracy in Europe fails.* Verlin: Argon Verlag, 2003

Paul van Buitenen. *Blowing the Wistle: Fraud in the European Commission.* London: Politicos, 2000

Philip Gounev, Vincenzo Ruggiero (eds.). Corruption and Organized Crime in Europe. London/New York: Rouledge, 2012.

Dirk Tänzler (ed.). The Social Construction of Corruption in Europe. Abingdon (GB): Ashgate, 2012 [on individual European countries].

In German:

Paul van Buitenen. Unbestechlich für Europa: Ein EU-Beamter kämpft gegen Misswirtschaft und Korruption. Gießen: Brunnen, 1999.

Sebastian Wolf. Korruption, Antikorruptionspolitik und öffentliche Verwaltung. Berlin: Springer VS, 2014.

Reference books and academic compendia

See all titles under "International" above.

Anke Butscher. "Corruption" University Bielefeld – Center for InterAmerican Studies, http://www.uni-bielefeld.de/cias/wiki/c_Corruption.html

Arnold J. Heidenheimer, Michael Johnston, M (ed.). Political Corruption: Concepts and Contexts. Transaction Publ.: New Brusnwick (NJ), 2002; Routledge: Abingdon, 2011

Paul M. Heywood (ed.) Routledge Handbook of Political Corruption. Routledge: Abingdon, 2014

In German:

Hans Herbert von Arnim (ed.). Defizite in der Korruptionsbekämpfung und der Korruptionsforschung. Berlin: Duncker & Humblot, 2009.

Britta Bannenberg, Wolfgang Schaupensteiner. Korruption in Deutschland: Portrait einer Wachstumsbranche. München: C. H. Beck, 2007^4.

Peter Graeff, Jürgen Grieger (eds.). Was ist Korruption? Baden-Baden: Nomos, 2012 [Members of the academic council of Transparency International Deutschland from various specialist disciplines].

Christian Höffling. Korruption als soziale Beziehung. Opladen: Leske + Budrich, 2002 [investigates 185 cases of corruption].

Stephan A. Jansen, Birger P. Priddat (eds.). Korruption: Unaufgeklärter Kapitalismus. Wiesbaden: VS Verlag für Sozialwissenschaften, 2005.

Sven Litzcke u. a. Korruption: Risikofaktor Mensch: Wahrnehmung – Rechtfertigung – Meldeverhalten. Wiesbaden: Springer VS, 2012.

Sebastian Wolf. Korruption (see under "Europe").

History

Ronald Kroeze, André Vitória, Guy Geltner (ed.) Anti-corruption in History: From Antiquity to the Modern Era. OUP: Oxford, 2017

Bruce Buchan, Lisa Hill. *An Intellectual History of Political Corruption*. Basingstoke (GB): Palgrave Macmillan, 2014.

Emmanuel Kreike, William Chester Jordan (ed.) Corrupt Histories. University of Rochester: Rochester, N.Y., 2004

Weitere Literatur zur Geschichte: https://www.u4.no/publications/historical-perspectives-on-corruption-in-europe.pdf

"Historical perspectives on corruption in Europe". https://www.u4.no/publications/historical-perspectives-on-corruption-in-europe

IV. Suggestions and Further Literature

In German:

Niels Grüne (ed.). Korruption: Historische Annäherungen an eine Grundfigur politischer Kommunikation. Göttingen: Vandenhoeck & Ruprecht, 2010.

Wolfgang Schuller (ed.). Korruption im Altertum: Konstanzer Symposium Oktober 1979. München: Oldenbourg, 1982.

The fight against corruption – law, institutional efforts

William P. Olson. The Anti-Corruption Handbook: How to Protect Your Business in the Global Marketplace. Wiley: Hoboken (NJ), 2010

Organization for Security and Co-operation in Europe. Handbook on Combating Corruption. OSCE: Vienna, 2016. https://www.osce.org/secretariat/232761

Ministry for Foreign Affairs of Finland, Department for Development Policy. Anti-Corruption Handbook for Development Practitioners. Heslinki, 2012. https://um.fi/documents/35732/48132/anti_corruption_handbook_for_development_practitioners

OECD, the United Nations Office on Drugs and Crime (UNODC), and the World Bank. Anti-Corruption Ethics and Compliance Handbook for Business. OECD: Paris, 2013, http://www.oecd.org/corruption/Anti-CorruptionEthicsComplianceHandbook.pdf

United Nations Office on Drugs and Crime. Anti-Corruption Ethics and Compliance Handbook for Business. UNODC: Vienna/New York, 2013

In German:

Texts from the German Federal Government:

http://www.bmi.bund.de/SharedDocs/Downloads/DE/Themen/OED_Verwaltung/Korruption_Sponsoring/jahresbericht-2014-korruptionspraevention.pdf?__blob=publicationFile.

http://www.bmi.bund.de/DE/Themen/Moderne-Verwaltung/Korruptio nspraevention-Sponsoring-IR/Korruptionspraevention/korruptionspraevention_node.html

Lukas Achathaler, et. al. (eds.). Korruptionsbekämpfung als globale Herausforderung. Wiesbaden: VS Verlag für Sozialwissenschaften, 2011.

Dirk Monsau. Vereinte Nationen und Korruptionsbekämpfung. Dresdener Schriften zu Recht und Politik der Vereinten Nationen 12. Frankfurt a. M.: Peter Lang, 2010.

Practical Steps for Fighting Corruption

Integrity Pacts. Transparency International. https://www.transparency.org/whatwedo/tools/integrity_pacts/3/.

Integrity Pacts in Public Procurement: An Implementation Guide. Transparency International. http://www.transparency.org/whatwedo/publication/integrity_pacts_in_public_procurement_an_implemen tation_guide.

International Whistleblower & Foreign Corrupt Practices Act Information. The Law Offices of Jason S. Coomer. http://www.internationalwhistleblower.com/in dex.htm.

Expolink Whistleblowing Hotline. Expolink. http://expolink.co.uk/ whistleblowing/.

https://whistleb.com/.

http://www.globethics.net/library/libraries-home.

Nissim Cohen. "Informal payments for healthcare – The phenomenon and its context." Journal of Health Economics, Policy and Law 7 (2012): 285–308, https://www.researchgate.net/publication/51109995_Informal_Payments_for_Healthcare-The_Phenomenon_and_ Its_Context

Evangelos Mantzaris u. a. "Interrogating Corruption: Lessons from South Africa". International Journal of Social Inquiry, 7 (2014): 1–17, https://www.researchgate.net/publication/319006717_Interrogating_Corruption_Lessons_from_South_Africa

http://www.iccgermany.de/fileadmin/user_upload/Content/Corporate_Responsibility___Anti-Korruption/RESIST.pdf.

Government of Lithuania. Anti-Corruption Handbook for Business. Vilnius, 2016. http://avv.stt.lt/portals/0/docs/AVV_EN.pdf

Martin T. Biegelmann, Daniel R. Biegelmann. *Foreign Corrupt Practices Act Compliance Guidebook.* Hoboken (NJ): John Wiley, 2010.

ICC Rules of Conduct and Recommendations to Combat Extortion and Bribery. http://www.iccwbo.org/Advocacy-Codes-and-Rules/Document-centre/2004/ICC-Rules-of-Conduct-and-Recommendations-to-Combat-Extortion-and-Bribery-(2005-Edition)/

ICC Guidelines on Agents, Intermediaries and Other Third Parties. http://www.iccgermany.de/fileadmin/user_upload/Content/Corporate_Responsibility___Anti-Korruption/ICC_Guidelines_on_Agents_Intermediariers_and_Other_Third_Parties.pdf.

ICC Rules on Combating Corruption. http://www.iccgermany.de/fileadmin/user_upload/Content/Corporate_Responsibility___Anti-Korruption/ICC_Rules_on_Combating_Corruption.pdf.

ICC Anti-Corruption Clause. http://www.iccgermany.de/fileadmin/user_upload/Content/Corporate_Responsibility___Anti-Korruption/ICC_Anti-Corruption_Clause.pdf.

ICC Guidelines on Gifts and Hospitality. http://www.iccgermany.de/fileadmin/user_upload/Content/Corporate_Responsibility___Anti-Korruption/ICC_Guidelines_on_Gifts_and_Hospitality.pdf.

IV. Suggestions and Further Literature

ICC Anti-Corruption Third Party Due Diligence: A Guide for Small and Medium Size Enterprises. http://www.iccgermany.de/fileadmin/user_upload/Content/Corporate_Responsibility___Anti-Korruption/ICC_Third_Party_Due_Diligence_Guide_for_SMEs.pdf.

"ICC Guidelines on Whistleblowing." http://www.iccgermany.de/fileadmin/user_upload/Content/Corporate_Responsibility___Anti-Korruption/ICC_Guidelines_Whistleblowing.pdf.

In German:

TI Integrity pact German: https://www.transparency.de/Integritaets pakt.80.0.html.

http://www.whistleblower-net.de/whistleblowing/

International Chamber of Commerce: German: http://www.iccgermany.de/standards-regelwerke/verhaltensrichtlinien/handlungsempfehlungen-zur-korruptionspraevention-und-bekaempfung/.

Uwe Bekemann. Kommunale Korruptionsbekämpfung. Stuttgart: Deutscher Gemeinde Verlag/Kohlhammer, 2007.

Dieter Dölling. Handbuch Korruptionsbekämpfung (see under "Law – German-speaking Countries").

Helmut Fiebig, Heinrich Junker. *Korruption und Untreue im öffentlichen Dienst: Erkennen – Bekämpfen – Vorbeugen*. Berlin: Erich Schmidt Verlag, 2004².

Peter Graeff, et. al. (eds.). *Der Korruptionsfall Siemens: Analysen und praxisnahe Folgerungen des wissenschaftlichen Arbeitskreises von Transparency International Deutschland*. Baden-Baden: Nomos, 2009.

Zora Ledergerber. „Whistleblowing" unter dem Aspekt der Korruptionsbekämpfung. Bern: Stämpfli Verlag, 2005.

Roder Odenthal. *Korruption und Mitarbeiterkriminalität*. Wiesbaden: Gabler, 2009⁴.

Ingo Pies. *Wie bekämpft man Korruption? Lektionen der Wirtschafts- und Unternehmensethik für eine ‚Ordnungspolitik zweiter Ordnung'*. Berlin: wvb Wiss. Verlag, 2008.

Raimund Röhrich (ed.). *Methoden der Korruptionsbekämpfung: Risiken erkennen – Schäden vermeiden*. Berlin: Erich Schmidt Verlag, 2008.

Good Governance

Good Governance. Wikipedia. https://en.wikipedia.org/wiki/Good_governance.

What is good governance? The Good Governance Guide. http://www.goodgovernance.org.au/about-good-governance/what-is-good-governance/.

Good Governance and Human Rights. http://www.ohchr.org/EN/Issues/Development/GoodGovernance/Pages/GoodGovernanceIndex.aspx.

http://www.ohchr.org/EN/Issues/Development/GoodGovernance/Pages/AntiCorruption.aspx.

Sam Agere, *Promoting good governance*. Commonwealth Secretariat: London, 2000

In German:

https://de.wikipedia.org/wiki/Gute_Regierungsf%C3%BChrung

http://www.bpb.de/apuz/28952/good-governance-gegen-armut-und-staatsversagen?p=all.

Franz Nuscheler. "*Good Governance: Ein universelles Leitbild von Staatlichkeit und Entwicklung?*". INEF-Report 96/2009,

http://inef.uni-due.de/page/documents/Report96.pdf.

Corruption in the church

Christoph Stückelberger. Corruption-free Churches. Geneva: Globethics.net, 2010; online http://www.globethics.net/documents/42 89936/13403252/FocusSeries_02_Corruption_Christoph_text.pdf.

In German:

German Evangelical Alliance, http://www.ead.de/die-allianz/auftrag/ werke-und-einrichtungen/grundsaetze-fuer-die-verwendung-von-spendenmitteln.html.

Evangelisches Missionswerk in Südwestdeutschland (EMS). Anti-Korruptions Policy. 2007. https://ems-online.org/uploads/media/EMS_Anti-Korruptions_Policy_deutsch.pdf.

Theodor Ahrens. "Wenn Gaben fehlgehen: Korruption als Problem ökumenischer Beziehungen," pp. 41-142 in: Theodor Ahrens (ed.). Vom Charme der Gabe. Frankfurt a. M.: Lembeck, 2008.

Christian efforts

Unashamedly Ethical. http://unashamedlyethical.com/

The Earth is the Lord's! Lausanne Movement. https://www.lausanne.org/content/lga/2015-07/the-earth-is-the-lords

Evangelicals Shine a Light on Corruption at the G20 Summit in Brisbane. World Evangelical Alliance, 2014. http://www.worldea.org/news/4494/evangelicals-shine-a-light-on-corruption-at-the-g20-summit-in-brisbane

Micah Statement on the Panama Papers and Corruption. World Evangelical Alliance, 2016. http://www.worldea.org/news/4681/micah-statement-on-the-panama-papers-and-corruption

In German:

http://www.jesus.ch/themen/kirche_und_co/kirchen_gemeinden_werke/265798-exposedkampagne_begruesst_g20massnahmen.html.

http://www.each.ch/sites/default/files/131209_COM_StopArmut_Antikorruption.pdf

https://www.kath.ch/medienspiegel/weniger-korruption-schafft-mehr-wohlstand/
http://www.micha-initiative.de/mitmachen/exposed
http://www.christnet.ch/de/content/mammon-dossier-20

The Bible and Christian Theology

Thomas Schirrmacher. Leadership and Ethical Responsibility: The Three Aspects of Every Decision. The WEA Global Issues Series. Vol. 13. Culture and Science Publishing: Bonn, 2013. http://www.bucer. org/resources/details/leadership-and-ethical-responsibility.html.

Geo-Sung Kim. Bridging Christianity and Anti-Corruption Movement: Christian Ethical Reflections on Sustainable Integrity System. A Dissertation Submitted to the Department of Theology and the Graduate School of Yonsei University in partial fulfillment of the requirements for the degree of Doctor of Philosophy. June 2009. http://www.transparency-korea.org/wp-content/uploads/2014/10/Dissertation_GSK.pdf

In German:

Paul Kleiner. Bestechung: Eine theologisch-ethische Untersuchung. Bern: Peter Lang, 1992.

Karl Rennstich. Korruption: Eine Herausforderung für Gesellschaft und Kirche. Stuttgart: Quell Verlag, 1990.

Karl Rennstich. Korruption und Religion. München: Rainer Hampp Verlag, 2005 (also all world religions).

Appendix: On German speaking countries (in German)

Germany

Bundeskriminalamt (BKA). Bundeslagebild Korruption, report 2014. https://www.bka.de/SharedDocs/Downloads/DE/Publikationen/Jahresberichte UndLagebilder/Korruption/korruptionBundeslagebild 2014.html.

KA. Bundeslagebild Korruption, report 2012. http://www.pro-honore.de/uploads/media/BKA_Bundeslagebild_Korruption_2012.pdf.

Transparency International Deutschland (annual reports of Transparency International in Germany). https://www.transparency.de/Publikationen.2175.0.html.

Hans Herbert von Arnim (ed.). *Korruption: Netzwerke in Politik, Ämtern und Wirtschaft.* München: Knaur, 2003.

Ludwig Greven. *Sind wir alle käuflich? Weshalb Korruption die Politik und unser Leben durchdringt.* Köln: Edition Lingen Stiftung, 2013.

Hans Leyendecker. Die große Gier: Warum unsere Wirtschaft eine neue Moral braucht. Reinbek: Rowohlt Tb, 2009.

Jürgen Roth, Rainer Nübel, Rainer Fromm. Anklage unerwünscht: Korruption und Willkür in der deutschen Justiz. Frankfurt a. M.: Eichborn, 2007; München: Heyne, 2008.

Werner Rügemer. Colonia Corrupta: Globalisierung, Privatisierung und Korruption im Schatten des Kölner Klüngels. Münster: Westfälisches Dampfboot, 2002[1]; 2012[7].

Frank Überall. Abgeschmiert: Wie Deutschland durch Korruption heruntergewirtschaftet wird. Köln: Bastei Ehrenwirth, 2011.

Switzerland

Transparency International Switzerland: http://www.transparency.ch/de/index.php?navid=1.

Frank Hertel. "Grösste Korruptionsfälle der Schweiz," GMX magazine, May 21, 2014. http://www.gmx.net/magazine/wirtschaft/groesste-korruptionsfaelle-schweiz-15468080.

Lukas Amstutz u. a. Die Schweiz, Gott und das Geld. Geneva: ChrisNet, 2013. http://christnet.ch/sites/default/files/Die%20Schweiz%2C%20Gott%20und%20das%20Geld.pdf.

Transparency International Switzerland. Korruption und Korruptionsbekämpfung in der Schweiz. 2013. http://www.transparency.ch/de/PDF_files/Divers/KorruptionSchweiz_Webversion.pdf.

IV. Suggestions and Further Literature

Transparency International Switzerland. Stiftung Ethos. Korruptionsbekämpfung in der Schweiz. 2011. http://www.transparency.ch/de/PDF_files/Divers/2011_Ethos_TI_D.pdf.

Transparency International Switzerland. Korruption im Sport. 2013. http://www.transparency.ch/de/PDF_files/Dossiers/Dossier_Sport_de.pdf.

Transparency International Switzerland. Politikfinanzierung in der Schweiz. 2012. http://transparency.ch/de/PDF_files/Dossiers/Dossier_Politikfinanzierung.pdf.

Austria

Transparency International Austria. https://www.ti-austria.at/.

Korruption in Österreich. http://www.wien-konkret.at/politik/korruption/.

Bundesamt zur Korruptionsprävention und Korruptionsbekämpfung, report 2014. http://www.bak.gv.at/cms/BAK_dt/download/downloads/files/Jahresberichte/BAK_Jahresbericht_2014.pdf.

Bundesjustizministerium für Justiz, Sektion Strafrecht. Korruptionsstrafrecht neu: Fibel zum Korruptionsstrafrechtsänderungsgesetz 2012. https://www.justiz.gv.at/web2013/file/2c948485398b9b2a013c6764c78f2bfb.de.0/korrstraeg_fibel_webversion.pdf.

Lukas Achathaler, inter alios, (eds.). Korruptionsbekämpfung als globale Herausforderung. Wiesbaden: VS Verlag für Sozialwissenschaften, 2011, esp. pp. 37-72.

Andreas Marco Stockhammer. Politische Korruption in Österreich. Diplomarbeit Universität Wien. 2011. http://othes.univie.ac.at/ 13474/.

Mafia, Human Trafficking

Francesco Forgione. Mafia Export. Munich: Goldmann, 2011.

Thomas Schirrmacher. Human Trafficking. The WEA Global Issues Series. Vol. 12. Culture and Science Publishing: Bonn, 2013. http://www.bucer.org/resources/details/human-trafficking.html.

Michael Jürgs. Sklavenmarkt Europa. Gütersloh: C. Bertelsmann, 2014.

Law – German-speaking countries

Thomas Ax, Matthias Schneider (eds.). Rechtshandbuch Korruptionsbekämpfung. Berlin: Erich Schmidt Verlag, 2010².

Dieter Dölling. *Handbuch Korruptionsbekämpfung: Für Wirtschaftsunternehmen und öffentliche Verwaltung.* Beck Juristischer Verlag, 2007.

Matthias Freund u. a. *Korruption und Kartelle bei Auftragsvergaben: Prävention – Sanktionen – Verteidigung.* C. H. Beck: München, 2008.

Pamela Linke. *Verknüpfung von Strafrecht und Steuerrecht zur Bekämpfung von Korruption im nationalen und internationalen Geschäftsverkehr.* Frankfurt a. M.: Peter Lang, 2011.

Reinhart Maurach, Friedrich-Christian Schroder, Manfred Maiwald. *Strafrecht Besonderer Teil Teilband 2: Straftaten gegen Gemeinschaftswerte.* Heidelberg: C. F. Müller, 2012, pp. 244-250, 347-361.

Roland Pfefferle, Simon Pfefferle. *Korruption im geschäftlichen Verkehr.* Stuttgart: Kohlhammer, 2011.

Ulrich Sommer. *Korruptionsstrafrecht.* Köln: Zap-Verlag, 2009.

Michael Ueberhofen. *Korruption und Bestechungsdelikte im staatlichen Bereich: Ein Rechtsvergleich und Reformüberlegungen zum deutschen Recht.* Freiburg: edition iuscrim, 1999.

Endnotes

1. Some historians claim that the most important dimensions of denazification occurred at an informal level, beginning in the 1960s when the younger generation asked members of the older generation, "What did you do during the war?" See, for example, Victor Sebestyen, review of Exorcising Hitler: The Occupation and Denazification of Germany by Frederick Taylor in The Guardian, 24 April 2011, https://www.theguardian.com/books/2011/apr/24/exorcising-hitler-germany-frederick-taylor.
2. For example, Ramsay MacMullen, Corruption and the Decline of Rome (Yale University Press, 1988).
3. Ovid (Publius Ovidius Naso), Metamorphosis, Book 1, lines 117 to 123; translated into English verse under the direction of Sir Samuel Garth by John Dryden, Alexander Pope, Joseph Addison, William Congreve and other eminent hands (London: Jacob Tonson, 1717; now: Internet Classics Archive, http://classics.mit.edu/Ovid/metam.1.first.html; originally published in Latin in the year 1 A.C.E.).
4. "Anti-corruption," March 10, 2016, The World Bank. http://www.worldbank.org/en/topic/governance/brief/anti-corruption.
5. Monsau, *Vereinte Nationen*, 1. We are using short versions of information about sources in many footnotes and retaining most of the original German format of footnotes. For complete publication information please see the bibliography.
6. "Corruption," *Special Eurobarometer no 397 (2014)*. http://ec.europa.eu/public_opinion/archives/ebs/ebs_397_en.pdf.
7. As cited by N. Rennstich, *Korruption: Eine Herausforderung*, 40.
8. Machtmissbrauch: Von destruktiver und von konstruktiver Macht," http://www.umsetzungsberatung.de/geschaeftsleitung/machtmissbrauch.php.
9. See Transparency International Schweiz, *Korruption und Korruptionsbekämpfung*, 29–33.
10. For further examples see Stockhammer, *Politische Korruption*, 58–72.
11. "U.S. Official Illegally Sold Visas Abroad." The Washington Post, February 8, 2003. http://candleforlove.com/forums/topic/1267-us-official-illegally-sold-visas-abroad/.
12. Fisman, *Gangsters*, 189–190.
13. For more on this theme see Meineke, *Korruption*, 141–165.
14. See Rennstich, *Korruption und Religion*.
15. For his own introduction to his formula see Robert Klitgaard, "International Cooperation against Corruption." *Finance & Development*, March 1998. http://www.imf.org/external/pubs/ft/fandd/1998/03/pdf/klitgaar.pdf.
16. See Höffling, *Korruption*, 14–18. He describes corruption as the symbolic concentration of everything that is evil.
17. Cited by Achathaler, *Korruptionsbekämpfung*, 131, 132.
18. Priddat, Schmid, *Korruption als Ordnung*, 63.

[19] https://www.bka.de/DE/UnsereAufgaben/Deliktsbereiche/Korruption/korruption_node.html.
[20] Bundeskriminalamt, *Bundeslagebild Korruption* 2012: 3.
[21] Pies, *Korruption*, 21.
[22] See Fredrik Galtung, "A Global Network to Curb Corruption: The Experience of Transparency International," in Ann M. Florini, editor. *The Third Force: The Rise of Transnational Civil Society*. Carnegie Endowment for Int'l Peace, 2012.
[23] Bundeskriminalamt, *Bundeslagebild Korruption* 2012: 8.
[24] Tranparency International, *Korruption und Korruptionsbekämpfung in der Schweiz*, 30.
[25] Forgione, *Mafia*, 35
[26] Transparency International, *"Global Corruption Report 2004,"* Pluto Press: London, 2004.
[27] See *Jahrbuch Korruption* 2006, 190–206.
[28] See Stückelberger, 56–61 and UNIFEM, UNDP, "Corruption, Accountability and Gender: Understanding the Connections. 2010," http://iknowpolitics.org/sites/default/files/undp-unifem_corruption2c20accountability20and20gender_en.pdf
[29] See Christine Schirrmacher and Thomas Schirrmacher, *Unterdrückte Frauen. Gewalt – Ausbeutung – Armut*.
[30] See info at http://de.wikipedia.org/wiki/Visa-Affäre.
[31] „Neue Schmiergeld-Affäre im Auswärtigen Amt," in *Spiegel Online*, 18. 12. 2010, http://www.spiegel.de/politik/deutschland/0,1518,735435,00.html.
[32] Laurence Cockcroft, *Global Corruption: Money, Power and Ethics in the Modern World*, London/New York: I. B. Tauris, 2012.
[33] See Fifka and Falke, *Korruption*, 151–167.
[34] Transparency International, *Money*.
[35] Transparency International provided expert input in their *Global Report* 2007, xxiv-xxvii.
[36] von Arnim, *Korruption* 58; see also 59–63.
[37] von Arnim collected a long list of documented acts of corruption in sports. See *Korruption*, 81–126.
[38] Transparency International Schweiz, *Korruption im Sport*, 2.
[39] http://www.gmx.net/themen/schweiz/top/8097j8w_p6-groessten-korruptionsfaelle-schweiz
[40] *Global Corruption Barometer 2013 – National results*. Transparency International, 2013. http://www.transparency.org/gcb2013/country/?country=germany, see also *Global Corruption Barometer 2017*.
[41] http://www.micha-initiative.de/mitmachen/exposed
[42] For a critical evaluation of the CPI see Jansen and Priddat, *Korruption*, 11–14; Litzcke, *Korruption*, 11–12; Fifka and Falke. *Korruption*, 123. For a discussion of the independence of TI see von Arnim *Korruption*, 127–150.
[43] https://www.transparency.org/news/feature/corruption_perceptions_index_2017#table.

44 "Bribe Payers Index 2011." Transparency International, 2011. http://www.transparency.org/bpi2011
45 "Bribe Payers Index 2011 — In detail." Transparency International, 2011. http://www.transparency.org/bpi2011/in_detail
46 http://www.transparency.org/news/pressrelease/20120710_ti_veroeffentlicht_transparenz_rangliste
47 "Global Corruption Barometer 2013." *Transparency International,* 2016. http://www.transparency.org/gcb2013
48 "*Corruption.*" Special Eurobarometer no 397. See footnote 1.
49 Bundeskriminalamt, *Bundeslagebild Korruption* 2012: 8.
50 See Dirk Holtbrügge and Carina B. Friedmann, *Geschäftserfolg in Indien,* Berlin: Springer, 2011.
51 For details see Rügemer, *Colonia.*
52 Johann Graf Lambsdorff, „Korruption als Wachstumsbremse," *Aus Politik und Zeitgeschichte* 2009, http://www.bpb.de/apuz/32249/korruption-als-wachstumsbremse?p=all; for more see Alemann, *Dimensionen,* 233-248.
53 More examples found in International Council on Human Rights, *Corruption and Human Rights.*
54 FAZ, 24. 03. 2014.
55 For more on this topic see Litzcke, *Korruption,* 38-40; Greaf and Grieger, *Korruption,* 156-158.
56 Bo Rothstein, *The Quality of Governance,* The University of Chicago Press, 2011, 193-206.
57 http://www.bak.gv.at/cms/BAK_dt/vorstellung/start.aspx
58 http://www.transparency.de/Integritaetspakt.80.0.html
59 http://www.icc-deutschland.de/icc-regeln-und-richtlinien/icc-verhaltensrichtlinien/icc-verhaltensrichtlinien-anti-korruption-bestechung-in-deutschland-definition-geschichte.html
60 See Litzcke, *Korruption,* 43-47; and Transparency International, *Whistleblowing in Europe.*
61 Bundeskriminalamt, *Bundeslagebild Korruption* 2012: 12.
62 http://www.whistleblower-net.de/was-wir-wollen/regelungen-in-organisationen/
63 See Van Buitenen, *Unbestechlich.*
64 The reports are summarized at http://www.europarl.europa.eu/experts/5_de.htm.
65 Deuteronomy 10:17
66 2 Chronicles 19:7
67 On the topic of corruption in the Bible and church history see Rennstich, *Korruption: Eine Herausforderung;* and Kleiner, *Bestechung.*
68 Micah 7:3
69 Micah 3:11
70 See also Stückelberger, *Corruption-free churches,* 125-126
71 Proverbs 21:14

[72] See also Klaus M. Leisinger, *Unternehmensethik: Globale Verantwortung und modernes Management* (C. H. Beck: München, 1997) 62–83. Leisinger distinguishes between minor corruption (often necessary to survive in the third world) and major corruption (though the distinction is not always clear), and, as we do, between corruption used for legally acceptable purposes (so that only the recipient is guilty) and corruption for illegal purposes (in which both parties are guilty).

www.ingramcontent.com/pod-product-compliance
Lightning Source LLC
Chambersburg PA
CBHW070323100426
42743CB00011B/2538